"This masterfully written and illustrated narrative strikes the bullseye dead on and arrives at a very important time. It will resonate on so many levels with readers, be they supporting someone dying, or dying themselves. A terrific read for me, as a senior oncologist and now a heavily invested patient."

John K. Erban, MD, Professor of Medicine, Tufts University School of Medicine, Former Clinical and Assoc Director for Clinical Research, Tufts Medical Center Cancer Center

"In this memoir, Lester thoughtfully captures the emotional roller coaster of the loss of two parents and one aunt. I practiced medicine for 31 years, but even so I learned and was touched, and, surprisingly, found great comfort in the way it helped me revisit, and reassess, the painful death of a close friend over a decade ago."

Thomas A. Tesoriero, MD, Retired Internist - Kaiser Permanente

"If you fear death or are in denial of the inevitable, this book is for you. Using the power of stories, poems, and art, Absolutely Delicious demonstrates with care and empathy the breadth of ways people can die on their own terms, and the impact that journey can have on their loved ones. Lester reminds the reader of the universality of death by offering an honest portrayal of three approaches to living one's last days, providing the space for each of us to consider our own priorities, helping to pave the way toward realizing our own compassionate end."

Kim Callinan, President and CEO, Compassion & Choices

ALSO BY ALISON JEAN LESTER

ABSOLUTELY DELICIOUS

A CHRONICLE OF EXTRAORDINARY DYING

by Alison Jean Lester

Illustrations by Mary Ann Frye

BENCH
PRESS

ISBN: 978-1-8381124-0-0 (Paperback)
ISBN: 978-1-8381124-1-7 (epub)

Illustrations by Mary Ann Frye
Front cover image by Mary Ann Frye
Book design by McPherson & Company

Excerpts from "As They Lay Dying" by Henry Mitchell from *The Washington Post*. © 1986 *The Washington Post*. All rights reserved. Used under license. "It's Never Too Late to Fall in Love", words and music by Sandy Wilson, Chappell Music Ltd (PRS), all rights administered by WC Music Corp.

First printing edition 2020

Published by Bench Press

alisonjeanlester.com

JOYFULLY FOR

AND WITH DEEPEST THANKS TO

VALERIE BROWNE LESTER

JAMES TRELOAR LESTER JR.

MARION JANE LESTER

Given the opportunity, dying deserves to be lived

with the same style one has chosen to live all the rest of the journey.

Death comes after life; dying is part of it.

– Thomas Hornbein
  Mountaineer and anesthesiologist
  Pioneer, with Willi Unsoeld,
  of the West Ridge ascent of Mount Everest
  Friend

Snow on the Great Wall
reminds me that there is light
even in winter

– Valerie Lester

CONTENTS

PREFACE

My mother, Valerie Lester, died on the morning of June 7, 2019, of metastatic melanoma. I'm driven to write about it because her death was, by all the standards I can imagine, a good one. Not only was the moment of her death good; the weeks of decline leading to her death were good. And not only that; the eighteen months between her first dire prognosis and her death were some of the happiest months of her life. Her final moment was, I suppose, ordinary – she drew a last breath, devoid of drama, when her body could no longer maintain itself. Her approach to dying, though? That was amazing.

I had the precious opportunity to be with her for the final two-and-a-half months of it, at first staying with her in her apartment, and then remaining there on my own and visiting her daily at the residential hospice facility she had chosen. I knew I'd want to write about the experience, just as I had written about the way my father had taken charge of the way he exited the world. I didn't have this book in mind right away, though. I started with haiku. Those tiny, intense poems were how my brain wanted to chronicle the residue of those days as I was living them.

Coyote trots past
Crow shadow climbs a fir tree
The food chain shimmers

(MAY 22)

I thought maybe I'd post the haiku on my Twitter feed, but recognized I didn't want the distraction of inviting people I didn't really know into the process. I do enjoy collaboration though, and emailed my mother's close friend Mary Ann Frye, whose amazing daily sketch journals I'd marveled at on many of my visits. She was also painting a portrait a day, and had done several of Mum over the years. Mary Ann was processing Mum's final months in images the way I was in words, so I proposed we do a book of haiku and sketches, either just for ourselves or for the wider world. This gave me a place to send the haiku right away, and an engaged witness in my quiet corner.

As the weeks with my mother passed, I found myself wanting to share much more, because a good death is hard to find. It's not unusual for people to consider it impossible. If a book about the ones I'd witnessed could help even one person, I'd be elated. If you are dying, or are supporting someone who is dying, I hope the experiences in this book will encourage, enable, and even entertain you.

I recognize that because Mum was nearly 80 and her children and most of her grandchildren are no longer children, she was spared the anguish of leaving very tender souls behind. Her husband was already dead, so she wasn't being wrenched away from a partner. There was no one she felt she needed to live *for*.

The blessing that she wasn't in pain went a very long way towards making her death a good one too, as did the fact that she suffered only minor side effects from the drugs she submitted to. However, I'm sure that if she had been in pain, she would have chosen not to suffer and have us watch her suffer for long. I think you'll see that too, once it's all been laid out.

First, a word from Mary Ann.

Alison explains my presence precisely. She invited me. She recognized that my sketches come from the same impulse as her haiku, to halt the mind where some strong awareness stopped the day, to mark the place and be able to find it again.

Valerie had a sparky genius – to waste nothing, to embrace fact, to be amused, to love just what life had on offer. While she breathed, she breathed. Puzzling over how to begin these drawings, I was inspired to see as she saw, with frank appetite and delight, as if I heard her voice and wit.

Here are three from my actual journals, where it always tickled Val to find herself.

2/25/17 Valerie made her
baklava, farewell meal,
6 weeks in Europe.

9/12/18 Rock whose gesture
recalls Val striding on the beach.

4/10/18 Valerie and Toby plan
to see the Grand Canyon, soon.

Valerie was one of the great friendships of my life. While she had her diagnosis in hand, I was doggedly moving from my seaside home and garden of 26 years. She brought sometimes three meals a week. I kept cutting garden bouquets for her. We shared an ethos akin to strenuous lap swimming by people who like to swim, walking the beach in storms by people who like to walk the beach.

Three stories about our friendship:

When I had not known Valerie long, she asked if Alison, whom I did not know at all, could be married in my garden. "Or is that too much to ask?" "Well, are they going to live with us after?" It was a gorgeous wedding, the only mild day in a heatwave and my glorious introduction to the whole family.

Deep into Valerie's diagnosis, she told me with uncharacteristic gravity that she so valued my loyalty. She said some people were staying away, she supposed out of fear. I said, "I'm not afraid." I enjoyed her company, and she had travelled so often during our ten-year relationship, that I calculated I was gaining the equivalent of years by seeing her several times a week while she was dying. About a week after she died and deeply sad, I was surprised by a flood of gratitude for her whole endeavor that still buoys me.

A third story makes me smile. Valerie dressed with fine instinct and flair, a gift to her community. In some bright dress, she grimaced and asked me, "Do I look like mutton dressed as lamb?" "Would you rather look like mutton dressed as mutton?" She would not.

I am honored and gratified to join Alison's quest to share her parents' lucid template. I am changed. I imagine any reader will be changed.

A.J.L. and M.A.F.
January 31, 2020

THE WOMAN

Mum was born in July of 1939, in the Wirral, England, and christened Valerie Jean Browne. Her English father, Hablot Robert Edgar Browne, was a civil servant working abroad in the British colonial government. Tall, lanky, very clean-cut, and with a look in photographs that he referred to, aptly, as "a sheep with a secret sorrow," her father was known to his friends as Phiz. He was the great-grandson of Hablot Knight Browne, who, as the family's original Phiz, illustrated the books of Charles Dickens for over two decades. My mother's vivacious, Scottish mother, Petra Elsie Tainsh, was an award-winning ballet and tap dancer until her marriage.

Mum was an only child. Her father hadn't wanted children, possibly because his mother had died of scarlet fever a few days after his birth. As Mum told it, her mother had been able to convince him to have just one when her doctor told her it would help clear up her skin. In the spring of 1940, my nine-month-old mother and my grandmother joined my grandfather in Barbados. They moved to Jamaica when Mum was four, and she experienced the happiest years of her young life. She had a passion for the ocean thereafter, and spent as little time as possible in landlocked places. She danced with great abandon and liked to cook 'rice and peas' and plantain at Christmas.

So many dramatic moves were decided for her in those days. Aged ten, she was deposited for a year with her maternal grandparents in Nottingham to get used to English life before attending boarding school. Her parents were moving to Nigeria and didn't deem it a good choice to bring her along. What she had to get used to, along with the lack of sun, was being humiliated by arriving at school with the petroleum jelly her

3

grandmother put in her hair, and being terrified when that same hair was set on fire by her cousin. Thirty years later the tensions and temptations of that distressing time came out in one of the first poems she wrote as an adult.

Pact

I swear to you, God, I will not do it,
Even though she makes me dry the dishes
Three times a day, and polish the glasses
With a silky cloth.

I promise you, God, I will not do it
Although she makes me dissect oranges
And grapefruit every night for breakfast
The following morning.

I will not do it, God, I swear to you
Although I go upstairs for her spectacles
Eleven times a day, and never get
To peel potatoes.

I promise you, God, I will not run
This carving knife through my grandmother.

After that year in Nottingham, she spent six years in a mediocre-at-best boarding school in Sussex. It was the first indication that her parents didn't deem her worthy of a fine education, but she strove for excellence there, and despite chilblains and frequent hunger, she distinguished herself in French and literature, winning medals from the Poetry Society for recitation. She was then sent to a 'finishing school' in Switzerland for a year, to perfect her French and her social graces, and improve her chances of finding a husband. It was a happy time for her; the girls spent their free time hiking and skating and skiing and smoking and eating cream and chocolate. When she returned to England, she lived with her parents in London, as her father had retired from the civil service. Her mother put her on a diet of celery.

Next up, not university but Mrs. Hoster's Secretarial College. Typing and shorthand – skills to work with, and, if you had itchy feet like hers, to travel with. She took herself back to Jamaica, setting off on the Cunard Line's R.M.S. *Media* across the Atlantic to New York in September 1959, and wrote to her parents from the ship:

I have made a rough assessment of those on board:
American (male and female) over sixty = about 80
*   "   "   "   "   " forty =   "   25*
English("   "   ") " sixty =   "   5
American (under 30) female   =   "   4
American male (eligible age)   =   NIL
English   "   "   "   =   "

She did find work in Jamaica, but she didn't stay long. Her letters home are in large part about drinks parties and gossip. She returned to England aged 21, but soon departed for Canada, encouraged by a boarding-school friend living in Montreal. I don't think moving to another country and working as a secretary was enough stimulation for her, though. She needed to keep moving, seeing, learning, and having fun. Also, she had fallen in some sort of love with Peter Anson, a captain in the Irish Hussars, whom she had met on the ship coming over. There was a flurry of visiting between Montreal and Kentucky, where he was on a training course, and a good deal of pressure to decide what to do because he was to be posted to Aden that November. As I understand it, when he didn't think it was a good idea to get married before he left, Mum decided he didn't really love her.

She trained as a Pan Am stewardess in the summer of 1962, and would be based in New York. She saw her Hussar in London during the relocation, but by this time she was dating someone else. Her wonderful, very English way with words shines out in her description of the situation to her parents in a letter of August 2nd that year:

[Anson] hadn't had breakfast, so we humped through to the dining
room where he ate the most smelly haddock in London at the time,
getting gloomier and gloomier with every bite, while I got brighter
and brighter thinking about Sally and Anne coming to see me. Then
we trailed round to the bus where he stood, upper lip getting very

long and making speeches about our always saying goodbye. I really
was stupefied – I can't think whether he has had a change of heart,
whether he has a streak of sadism or whether he is just plainly fond
of me! What do you think? Anyway on getting back to New York I
find the whole place painful without Dick, so I think your daughter
has a case of not knowing her arse from her earhole and right now I
couldn't begin to tell you which I preferred!*

*Dick or Anson not my arse or my earhole!

She wore Pan Am blue for eighteen months, and had a ball. Why such a short career, if she was enjoying it? She met my father, Jim Lester, on a plane. A jazz-playing, photograph-taking psychologist twelve years her senior who had escaped Missouri for the world, he was traveling to London to stay with his sister, Jane, having participated in the first American expedition to Mount Everest, in 1963. In July 1963 Mum wrote to her parents: "Jim is without question the most wonderful thing that has ever happened to me – particularly at this time, and has proved so many things to me that everything seems quite clear." My parents were married in London in early 1964. My brother, Toby, was born in San Francisco in late 1964. I surprised them in Los Angeles in 1966.

I often wonder how many people have the opportunity to watch a parent develop the way I did.

In 1979, when she was forty, Mum started writing poems. Memories and emotions began to pour out of her, beginning with the story of how my brother had been taken from her straight after his birth for fear of infection, and how she had worried that they wouldn't bond. She wrote about the surgery he had to have at three months. She wrote about Jamaica and Nottingham. She wrote about Dad.

On Timing

The night before the day
Before the moon was full
I said to Jim,
"If you go first,
"I'll kill myself."

"I must be careful, then,"
He said
"To coincide my dying
"With a tiny moon;
"That slim, celestial paring
"You spoke of yesterday."

He never says,
"If you go first,
"I'll kill myself."
He naturally assumes
It's in his stars
To leave before me.
He came before me after all,
And had a decade to himself.
So I will have a tenner, too,
Or so he thinks.

But I don't want those years
All by myself –
Those years of marrow-cold
And spine down curving
And wanting energy
Without him.

Couldn't we, Jim,
Hold hands and step into the light
Together?

We had moved to Massachusetts by then, after spells in St. Croix and London, and she was taking classes in the continuing education program at Harvard, able to do so for free because she was working as a secretary at the university. She flirted with the idea of a degree in the history of science. I think it was when the words started flowing that she shifted to taking classes in English literature, and especially poetry. It was Mum who taught me to take rejection as a writer, back in those pre-Internet days. "You've got to have the envelope all ready and waiting for the next place you want to send your work to," she said. "When the poem comes back, you just put it in that envelope and send it right back out."

Dad had known all along that he'd married a woman who was intelligent as well as beautiful and funny. Now Mum was learning to see herself that way as well.

When my parents moved from Massachusetts to Washington, DC, Mum took a job as secretary to the chief medical resident for the coordination of the internal medicine residency training at the George Washington University School of Medicine, and finished her BA at GW. She followed that up with an MA from Georgetown University, which she pursued full-time, and before long she was teaching various courses at GW, including humanities and poetry versification. I have a syllabus from a versification class she taught in 1994, which would have given her students a very good idea of how unconventional she was. In week one, the subject was rhythm and the subtitle was "Start with your heart: kaBOOM kaBOOM. kaBOOM kaBOOM." In week 12, they looked at free verse: "Back home again, in the twentieth century. Hang out with modern poets. Find your favorites. Figure out how they do it, how they get away with being so free – and are they? Are you?"

Good manners were extremely important to her, but so was swearing. I think I was in my early teens when she told me, "There's nothing quite as good as a well-placed 'fuck'." She loved provoking me and others to speechlessness. Part Mary Poppins and part Monty Python, she swung between the two like Tarzan between vines. Her Britishness was obvious to everyone because of her accent, but she loved being American. Her father, unmoved by his daughter's desire to vote in her adopted country, had objected to her becoming a U.S. citizen, seeing it as disloyal. But the U.S. had been a land of great opportunity for her, and she didn't imagine leaving. She eventually became a citizen behind his back, and her mother kept her secret.

When Mum's father died after many years of Parkinson's disease, in the summer of 1986, she wore one of his singlets under her clothes for days. They had a tremendous amount of unfinished business, as she had not felt particularly loved by him. He seldom wrote to her, seldom visited her at boarding school and never for long. She told me that at school she had told herself that fathers loved their daughters, that was a fact, so he must love her, however he behaved. Wearing that droopy singlet, she forced a hug out of him.

In among my grandmother's papers, which I brought home after Mum died, is a letter to her from Mum on the envelope of which Granny wrote 'KEEP' in orange magic marker and 'VERY SPECIAL' in red ballpoint. Enclosed with the letter is an article cut out of *The Washington Post*. My mother wrote, "As I read this article, all I could do was think of you, and realized what a fitting tribute it is to all you achieved. I found the final paragraph especially moving and appropriate." The clipping is a column by Henry Mitchell and is titled "As They Lay Dying". In it he is disgusted by his perception of the attitude of many Americans to death:

> In America, where the influence and effect of public glop must be greater than anywhere else, from the White House through the media through the marrow of our bones, we attach incredible importance to how we feel and what our consciousness is. We believe, either secretly or openly, that if we feel good we're on the right track – like those morons who used to think the smell of roses would cure everything.

He goes on to say that when it comes to caring for the dying, "What counts – and in this alone the Puritans were always right – is will and a fire that won't go out." Later he exhorts: "Make up the mind what the work is, that is to be done, and do it in anger, in disgust, in whatever feeling arises, keeping as firm a control over the expression of these feelings in the presence of the sick as possible. But do it and keep on doing it until the end. That is not what good feelings are about, but it is what love is about."

My grandmother had cared for her ailing husband for as long as she was physically able, and when she could no longer manage, she took the decision to move him to a nursing home, unfortunately called the British Home and Hospital for Incurables. He was so offended by this move that he turned his face to the wall, and died without forgiving her.

In the final paragraph of Mitchell's column, the one Mum felt paid tribute to her grieving, guilt-ridden mother's effort, he writes:

Even in prolonged cases, even with boredom and disgust, there
are rewards along the way of humor and delight. Good days.
There may even be (for some say God is in the plan) Mozart
on the day of death, and quiet breathing. Those who have
given such care, with all their energy and will and such faltering
grace as they can manage, have a reasonable and basalt pride,
having given up so many concerts, as you might say, to play gin
rummy with those whose minds are failing (down to gin rummy,
actually) and whose bodies are full of offense. Except to love.
Let's make that (lest it be confused with something less) except
to Love.

My grandmother's Alzheimer's disease led to her London apartment
being covered in a flurry of Post-it-Note reminders and frying food being
left to catch fire on the stove. Being an only child, Mum had to make all
the decisions around her mother's care. I observed Mum's anxiety when
she had a trip to England coming up, and her efforts to get herself in
the right frame of mind. I listened to her call her friends to confer and
console and be consoled, as many of their parents were in decline and
dying as well. I remember thinking that if my parents died in old age, I
also wouldn't be alone in going through it.

My grandmother didn't turn her face to the wall when my mother moved
her to a care home, formerly a country mansion, up in Cheshire. She
herself had initiated the move, asking my mother, after yet another kitchen
fire, "Isn't there somewhere I can go?" Once settled in, Granny seemed
happy enough, and convinced herself that she had attended dances there
as a girl. When I visited her, she didn't recognize me, and during dinner
took her dentures out and put them on her plate, forgot what they were,
and tried to eat them, but she wasn't exhibiting distress. She still had good
energy, and on a very memorable walk together we skipped along chant-
ing a rhyme that went with our steps: "I left my luggage in a left-luggage
locker and I came right back to get it. But the luggage that I left in the
left-luggage locker wasn't right where I had left it."

Granny eventually died of a series of strokes. Mum flew to be with her at
the beginning of the end, just before her final master's degree exams were
about to start. She kept notes of her days there: "11/24 She's had her bath.
She's talking. She's weepy. I sit beside her. We're both in chairs. I ask her
if she'd like some music. She says: 'Yes, please.' I put on 'My Fair Lady'.

When we get to 'Wouldn't it be Loverly?' she stands up. I hold her hands and, in some sense of the word, we dance."

It was impossible for the nurse to say exactly how much time Granny had left, but she didn't make it sound immediate. Mum took a chance in flying home to sit the exams. Three days later her mother died.

Mum told me in her final months that not being there at the time of her mother's death had always haunted her. Hope springs eternal, though, and I find it easy to understand her determination to achieve the education that had been denied, willing with all her might for the stars to align in her favor.

After Granny was gone, Mum felt her spirit return with wings.

Revenant

After my year of grieving, after all
my one-way conversations, you
could not resist that call,
that place, that view,
that pull,
pull I
exerted on
your curiosity.
That night, right after all the song
and my return to bed, I saw you. I

know it was you, my mother, Luna moth-
disguised, gorgeous, in green of life
whispering, soft as breath
"Sleep well, sleep safe.
No death
can tear
me from you. Look
at me. I'm everywhere:
I'm sky, I'm sea, I'm tea, I'm book,
I'm rock, I'm wine, I'm cloth, I'm soap, I'm air."

(OCTOBER 1993)

Mum began her book-writing career with a history of Pan Am Airlines, and went on to make a name for herself as a biographer. I will talk more about that in "The Notebook". For now, I want you to think back to that early poem, "On Timing", where my mother told my father that she'd kill herself when he died. That was something she said to me from time to time as well, although there was a period when she talked about going to Buenos Aires to learn to tango instead. When he did contract a disease and die, she pursued neither of these things. She was in the middle of a biography that she had put on hold to care for him, and he had made her promise that she would finish it. Maybe he was truly worried that she was serious about doing away with herself, but I think it's much more likely that he felt guilty about having kept her from an interesting project for so many months. She took up the project again, and made a great success of it.

I know she didn't begrudge the time she spent caring for Dad, initially on her own and later with the help of nursing aides and hospice. She had spent 46 years with him, and living through his way of dying paved her own path of acceptance, appreciation, amazement, and even amusement, when her time came.

ANOTHER WORD FOR IT

In April of 2010, my 82-year-old father committed suicide. I mean that in the best possible sense. The event was so elegant, so charitable, as to beg the question of whether or not suicide is the right word. If suicide is the act of killing oneself intentionally, then it's wide of the mark. There was no action involved. He simply stopped eating and drinking.

He had ALS, amyotrophic lateral sclerosis. Some know it as Lou Gehrig's Disease, others as motor neurone disease.

Dad had nothing to say about the afterlife except that he didn't believe in it. He accepted the aging process, and didn't seem to fear death. It was hard to say why. After he died though, my mother gave me a manuscript that he had written before I was born, and it revealed thoughts I hadn't been aware of.

Dad had participated in the American Mount Everest Expedition in 1963, studying the dynamics of the group under stress. Once back, he wrote his experience of the climb as a story for young readers – kids of about 12 or so. In it, he described his response to the death of the team's youngest member, Jake Breitenbach, who was crushed while trying to map a route through the Khumbu icefall. While the event was shocking, and forced the team to reflect and reconsider over several days, my father wrote: "That one light should go out here did not seem so surprising or wrong as it does at home, where all the forces seem to be under control and life seems so safe. In the mountains I felt clearly that human life is just one among many other things going on in the world, and that it is in constant struggle with many other things and that it sometimes must lose the struggle."

It's hard to imagine that his philosophical approach wasn't linked to these early feelings. I've never met someone so philosophical. "I'm old enough," he said to Ron Hoffman, the indefatigable founder of Compassionate Care ALS, who came by frequently in the last months of Dad's life, dropping off donations of equipment and speaking his support for ways to live with the paralyzing disease. Ron generously kept delivering things that would make it easier for Mum and the hospice nurses to move Dad around, but no harnesses or transfer aids could wipe away the crystal clarity of the statement Dad wrote even before his diagnosis: "I've lived long enough and feel no need to cling to a life from which many of the functions that make for quality have been removed. My condition would not have to be terminal to make me want to have an end to it."

So that was it. And that had always been it.

Less than a year before his death, my parents moved from their house in Maryland to a wonderful 'senior living community' in Hingham, Massachusetts called Linden Ponds. I spent a few weeks helping them pack, and found myself in the back room by the washing machine with Dad, filling and labeling boxes with 50 years of slides, and discussing the use of helium in assisted suicide. He had a video about it on a shelf. I don't recall that he asked me what I thought about the helium option; he just told me he was thinking about it. It was attractive because filling the plastic bag over your head with helium prevents the panic that accompanies suffocation, and also because the direct cause of death is difficult to trace if the bag and gas canister are disposed of before the death is reported. It was unattractive because you couldn't do it alone. Depending on your condition you might be able to manage the equipment before death, but someone would have to get rid of it. He didn't like the idea of involving us more than necessary. He was still thinking.

Before they got in the car on the day they left for Massachusetts, my mother took Toby and me into the empty kitchen. Her eyes were full of tears, but she wasn't desperate. "He's probably going to do this," she said. "I don't know how he's going to do it, or when, but he's probably going to. Just so you know." Toby and I nodded at her. We knew.

Dad was able to drive all the way to their new home, where there were no stairs to negotiate and all the hallways had handrails, but a few months later they narrowly avoided a car accident when he couldn't lift his foot off the accelerator. He declined very quickly from the Charles Eames-esque armchair to the Barcalounger, from the Zimmer frame to the electric wheelchair. His voice on the phone became more and more slurred. He couldn't swallow easily, trying to clear the phlegm in his chest made him gag, and defecation was a nightmare. I flew over at Christmas with my fiancé, now husband, Andy, so they could meet. I flew back over in March. That was when Dad had Toby and me watch a video of a man, terminally ill with cancer, who makes the choice to end his life through fasting. It was a beautiful video, and a terrible moment. Dad had made his decision. He was just worried about one thing.

As a psychologist, Dad spent his professional time trying to make sense of things. He wasn't assertive, and his modest nature had him seeing both sides of a lot of human issues. This meant that he could imagine people seeing his choice to fast to death as wimping out. He expressed this concern a lot. It was amazing to me that he thought there were only a couple of ways to see his decision, i.e., wimpy or courageous. We were overwhelmed by how many friends were struck by his courage. There was only one person who kept up an active dialogue with him about how he could stay alive for longer, and that was Ron Hoffman. It was Ron's business to get people with ALS the resources they needed – the right commode, the right shower chair, the right foam supports, the right oxygen therapy. He didn't want someone to feel like they couldn't go on living just because they hadn't been offered the special harness that could get them in and out of bed. Dad didn't want to disappoint Ron, but it was precisely because he was at the stage of needing equipment for every single activity of every single day that he made his decision.

You can see the way he was weighing up the value of his life in a statement he wrote as he was preparing for the end (preparing us, that is, not himself): "I'm happy with my life as I lived it: I've passed my 82nd birthday and my 46th wedding anniversary with as fine a wife and lover as anyone could want, I've watched my two children grow into wonderful, productive adults and give me 5 grandchildren, I've loved and been loved, admired and been admired, achieved a few things and experienced a lot, and I can survey the whole with rich feelings of contentment and satisfaction." Surveying the future, he had this to say: "What I want to avoid is unnecessary and prolonged suffering purely for the sake of prolonging life regardless of its quality." He looked at the bills he received for all the tests and procedures he had undergone, and shook his head in dismay. Medicare would pay for them, sure. But that was precisely why he felt the pain. I'd call Dad very much a JFK Democrat, and I believe he maintained his connection to the values of that era. Allow people to live the way they see fit. Do what you can for your country. It was abhorrent to him that the American taxpayer was to be saddled with maintaining the meager delineations of the last years of his life. So, setting the past and the future side by side, in much the same sensible way that he had compared purchase options in his exhaustive research of any used car or new fridge, he made the choice that satisfied his logic: not to allow the last months of his life to be so completely unlike his life as to eclipse it.

"Here's how I want you to remember me," he said when he could still talk intelligibly, handing me a photo of him in his 50s, grinning in a top hat. It's funny, because that photo doesn't really remind me of him. He had a great sense of humor, but he wasn't a goofball. He was modest. He played beautiful jazz piano and trombone. He spent the bulk of his career, after early days of clinical psychology and teaching, in the Office of Naval Research, administering grant money for research in the behavioral sciences. He wasn't happy working there, particularly as the presidential administrations became more conservative and grant money for the soft sciences was harder and harder to come by. But he kept playing jazz and taking photos during the evenings and weekends, and when he retired, wrote a biography of the jazz pianist Art Tatum. *The Washington Post*'s Jonathan Yardley said of it, "Among the spate of jazz biographies that have been inflicted upon us in recent years, *Too Marvelous for Words* stands out from the crowd."

I know that my father was deeply depressed at times in his life. I know that he questioned his musicianship and wished he'd been able to sell more photos. He wrote drafts of two more books – one a historical look at why mountaineers climb, one a biography of Timothy Leary. He didn't find a publisher for the first, and Robert Greenfield beat him to it on the second. But when he wasn't feeling frustrated, he found great pleasure in both big events and poignant moments, and these piled up and outweighed the advantages of staying alive for the sake of it. When he could no longer play the piano, when he could no longer hold a camera or a conversation, what then were his struggles to chew, swallow and breathe in aid of?

For my mother, disagreeing with his choice was never an option, but while she would not be required to participate actively in his death, her support was making it possible. He couldn't do it without her. "I feel that I'm your executioner," she told him. "No," he said. "You are my hope."

Dad stopped eating and drinking on April 16th, 2010. When Andy and I arrived from Singapore on the night of the fourth day of his fast, he was sitting up in his chair in the living room. He looked gorgeous. A nurse's aide was coming in every day to bathe him, so his hair was clean and his beard snowy. His cords and turtleneck looked great on his lanky frame. At that moment, he was still very Dad.

His sister arrived as well, and stayed in a nearby apartment with Andy and me. Toby stayed in the apartment with Mum, in case she needed help in the night.

It was sunny during the days, and for the first few we were able to take him out to a nearby pond and sit and chat while he dozed in the sun. When he was visibly much weaker, we moved him to the hospital bed that fit into the bay window in the living room. He could no longer reach for the swab that kept his mouth moistened, so we took turns swabbing his mouth and putting lip salve on his lips. The hospice nurse showed us how to administer syringes of palliative medicine under his tongue, both for breathing problems and for anxiety. He looked out the window. He listened to jazz. He winked at us. For the first few nights we looked at selections from the slides he'd been taking since the 1950s, literally making his life pass before his eyes. Many times on those evenings, he was the one who was able to put to rest a lot of questions about who was who in the photos, and where they were.

Photos of him during those days, and even from the few months before the decision, show a man who had already started leaving his life. We kept taking them, in different groupings, outside by the pond, inside gathered around his chair. Looking back on it, I can't really think why. His body had been telling the story of his death for over a year, but when his face started joining in, he had reached the point of no return. It's much too hard to look at those photos now, but it did help to look into his eyes during those moments. They made it clear that he was fighting to stay with us, and just needed our permission to push off.

One of the things I was really glad the hospice people told us was that dying people can act in ways you've never seen. It's not something I've heard talked about much. It makes sense, of course, but not the sense I thought it made. I could easily imagine that my dad might become fretful over his decision, or morose, or angry, but Ron told me to be prepared because he might suddenly try to do something like pinch my mother's bum. He couldn't say exactly what he'd do, just that he would most likely do something. And he did. He became fixated on needing to pee.

By the time this happened, it had been a week since he'd had anything to drink other than the water that dripped down his throat after we swabbed out his mouth (even when he seemed to be sleeping his mouth would reflexively chew on the swab). He also had an adhesive catheter on, so if there were any urine in his bladder he could let go. He was determined to get up, though, and his arms would flail as he tried to sit upright and pull his legs over the side of the bed. We'd have to stand right next to the bed and block his efforts with our bodies, speaking soothingly. Eventually he'd give up and shrug his shoulders in a "Have it your way, asshole" manner that didn't resemble Dad at all.

Every day had some peace, every day had anxious moments. I believe in this case we are fortunate to be a very small family, which meant that we could all be there, and could all find a role to play. We fell into a rotation through a list of tasks and responsibilities, and I would recommend this to any family approaching a similar event. In order not to distress a starving man with the smell of food, we avoided cooking in the apartment as much as possible, and ate in the residence cafeteria or café. One of us would stay with him while the rest of us ate out, and we'd bring them back a sandwich or a salad. We took turns administering his drugs and swabbing his mouth. We took turns reading or singing to him. And we took turns going out for relief – a massage, a walk in the woods, a bike ride. I don't know how people can manage this if they are too numerous, or not in agreement. I shudder to think. But it does seem to me that our family's ability to function smoothly during those days stemmed from my father's having made his values clear to us for many, many years.

If your parents or partners have not been vocal about the end of their lives, I'd say ask. Do it. It's hard. And it's good. Andy and I did it soon after he met my dad, walking between sunny, snow-covered fields in his native England. I won't forget the conversation, but I'll also insist on having it again, just to see if anything's changed. If his thoughts have shifted I want to know, so I can help him both to live and to die in the way he desires to.

The last real conversation Dad had was with my mother, about four days before he died. She came in from an errand and said, "Hello darling, I'm here," and he said, "I'm not." When she asked him if everything was all right, he said, "Ideal."

On the eleventh night of Dad's fast, none of us wanted to leave him. It was something we agreed on almost without discussing it. Mum slept in the chair by Dad's bed in the living room, with Toby on the floor. Andy and I were in the bedroom on one side of the living room, and my aunt was in the den on the other.

Something woke my mother and brother shortly before six the next morning. Neither of them can say what it was, but both of them went straight to Dad. He wasn't breathing, but he was still warm. He still had color. Mum woke me up, and I went out and felt his warmth as well. Andy joined us and went to wake up my aunt. We all stood around his bed, watching, listening, seeing his skin go pale, relieved that he was no longer struggling to breathe, and overwhelmed by his timing. He had only just died. He had let us all sleep through the night, and everyone we needed to call was awake, or soon to be.

Dad's hospice nurse came and pronounced him dead. When she was gone, my mother invited my aunt and me to join her in washing his body. Again, we easily found our places, with Mum and me on either side and my aunt at his feet. Later, Andy noted how we reacted when Dad died. "It was like you all just went, 'Oh!'" he said. And he was right. It was a quiet moment. There was no more ragged breathing, there were no more false alarms. But like everyone else in the world faced with a peaceful loved one lying quietly in bed, I didn't know how to register him as gone. Bathing him helped with that. Mum was washing his face, and I was washing his chest. The center of his chest was a bit scaly, and I wanted it clean and smooth, so I scrubbed a bit, and as I scrubbed his chest hair came out into the washcloth. "Oh," I thought again, differently this time. I rinsed the washcloth and finished washing his chest and arm, more gently. We noticed the livor mortis in his heels and back. Toby and Andy stepped in to help dress him in his most comfortable nightshirt, and we covered him in a quilt made by a friend. Mum called the undertaker.

There's a story attributed to the Chinese philosopher Laozi about some very old men who gather every morning outside their village huts in order to sit and chat. One morning, one of the old men, whose bones are twisted with arthritis, comes out of his hut and sees his shadow thrown onto the wall by the rising sun. "Hey!" he laughingly shouts to his friends, "I look like a chicken!"

When I told this story to my father, well before he was sick himself, he laughed so hard tears came to his eyes. He loved that old man, a perfect, uplifting representation of the Taoist concept of *wu wei*, or non-action. These Chinese words are also variously rendered by Alan Watts in his book *The Watercourse Way* as not doing anything, not forcing, creating nothingness, acting spontaneously, and flowing with the moment.

I think maybe this, and not suicide, is what Dad committed.

PREPARATION

So, we had Dad's approach to taking control of the end of his life as a guide.

That didn't mean that it was easy to accept that Mum was terminally ill. I was very surprised that she was going to die at all. It hadn't really occurred to me, even though she'd had an operation to remove a malignant mole and some lymph nodes in her groin. I didn't truly connect the fear I experienced discovering a lump in my breast with the fear she had been living with for a few years already.

I felt the lump in a hotel in London in 2014, en route from Singapore to Massachusetts. I'd fallen out of the habit of feeling for lumps after I hit menopause, since the last day of each period had been a reminder to lie down and do a breast exam. Also, I usually washed myself with one of those scrunchy things that scrub your skin, but in our London hotel I was washing with my hands, and suddenly could feel the change to my landscape. I called Mum, and she made me an appointment with her physician.

In between that appointment and one with Mum's oncologist, Mum took me to a yoga class at the Y. "Terrible teacher," she said, "but it's a lovely stretch." Sometimes in those days I did a few moon salutations at home, but usually in the half dark of early-morning Singapore. In the bright light of late-morning Massachusetts, I pressed into downward dog and regarded the state of my legs. The skin was bunched and crinkled around the knees, hanging loose and tired along the thigh, with an alarming dimple, in no way cute, on the right side. Death Valley National Park sprang to mind. I had clearly come to the end of elasticity. I knew that already, more or less. I have more of a natural frown these days, but I can smile to fix that. When I sleep on my side, there are vertical creases between my breasts at breakfast, but they disappear by about lunchtime. The only way I could see to remedy the Downward Dog Situation, though, was to build my thigh muscles to a point where they'd take up all the slack. Thing is, I'd usually rather write a book.

During that yoga class, I remembered another class, about fifteen years before, where the teacher's voice was North Indian gentle as opposed to Southeast Massachusetts harsh ('hahsh'). That teacher reminded us as we stood in the mountain pose to be thankful for our bodies: for our two perfect feet and our two perfect legs that helped us move through the world, carrying our souls where they wanted to go. Too often, she told us, our desires made us drag our bodies around, wearing them out, denying them the respect they deserved. "So let us thank them."

Still in downward dog, I could see my mother between my shins. She was nearly 75, and believed yoga was helping to slow the shrinking she felt herself doing, and developing her balance. She was well aware that when old ladies fell over, it was frequently the beginning of the end. We lost my father's mother to a punctured lung when she tumbled on the stairs and broke a rib.

A few days later, my mother, my husband and I took the ferry that crosses the bay to Boston and walked the rest of the way to the doctor who had removed the melanoma from Mum's left thigh two years before. I had an appointment with him at 9:00 and an ultrasound slated for 9:30, a mammogram for 10:00. In the end, though, the whole visit took about fifteen minutes. The doctor found the lump easily (it was a doozie). He told us that the other procedures required too much paperwork, and anyway, "I'm a needle guy." Then he left the room.

Andy and I had imagined that we might be given a choice in the matter, and when the doctor came back, he noticed our surprise. "People like to use digital guidance these days," he said, "but I've been using my hands for years. This won't hurt a bit." He stuck the needle in, and almost right away smiled and said, "It's a cyst."

The liquid was a muddy green. I felt like an alien. "It's either this muddy green, or a sort of light beer," he told me. He visually assessed the color, confirmed it was healthy, and tossed the syringe in the bin. Done. He shook our hands and left again. I burst into tears. Andy and I both needed a good long hug.

I brought the joy back into the waiting room, and received kisses from my mother, who had been through the same breast-related turmoil three times herself. We went down to the payment center, and then, after listening to the whole story of the finance officer's wedding in Scotland and seeing a photo of her 81-year-old husband (she was 55), we practically skipped out of the building.

My skin has lost its elasticity, but it's not a skirt. I can still wear it. It still protects the flesh my blood flows through, the muscles that can sprint if necessary, the bones that stand tall and keep moving. We strode along the sidewalk, my mother and I, our legs scissoring forward, throwing long shadows on the outer edge of the valley of death.

We'd avoided the worst, we thought. But in fact, only I had. She was approaching that golden date of five years without an issue, feeling very optimistic, but just before the five-year mark Mum was back at the oncologist, needing more lymph nodes removed. That put her back on more frequent check-ups, and a scan revealing cancer in her liver. She was told to expect to start feeling rotten in about six months.

It surprised both Toby and me that she had to be convinced to undergo a course of immunotherapy even though her melanoma specialist, Donald Lawrence, MD, was very optimistic about her chances. Then again, she had often said she didn't fancy living to 80, and she had terrible 'white-coat syndrome'. Her blood pressure skyrocketed when she had to go see a doctor, no matter how nice they were. She liked and appreciated all her doctors, from her GP at Linden Ponds to Dr. Lawrence at Mass General Hospital, but on the days when she had appointments she would pace and fret, and when they took her blood pressure their eyebrows would fairly fly off their faces. Toby was privy to most of this anxiety, as Mum would drive to his and spend the night if she had an early appointment in Boston. He asked her about it. Apparently the fear went way back into childhood, to the extent that her mother would keep upcoming doctor appointments a secret, taking her out on some other pretext. Then, when they were passing the doctor's office, Granny would whisk her inside and close the door. Which must have helped a lot.

Not.

She was eventually convinced to give immunotherapy a try, every three weeks between January 5th and March 16th, 2018. She fortunately had none of the side effects that some people find intolerable. She had no side effects at all, in fact, other than anxiety before every session. But Toby and her friends jollied her along, taking turns driving her either to the hospital or to the train into Boston, and she got through it.

Still, we couldn't assume that how well she felt meant she was cured, no matter how much we wanted to. Those months were very hard to bear.

Spring's Ankle Boots

Spring's ankle boots are in
(I read)
and they're really pretty!
I pretend the headline refers to
snowdrops
like the ones at the foot of
my apple tree.
My apple tree, I say,
as if the relationship were permanent.
It's a temporary union,
no matter how long
I keep this house.
My mother, I say,
many times a day,
as if that were permanent too.
My mother.
My mother is ill.
My mother.
My mother.
My mother will die,
whether or not she is cured,
and so will the snowdrops,
and all the cows people need
to look pretty.

(FEBRUARY 2018)

I went to the States in April to be with her during the scans that would show the effect of the therapy, and both Toby and I accompanied her to the hospital for the results the next day. In the waiting area we sat behind a crumpled, striving young man whose mother ceaselessly massaged his shoulders. A stickman in a peach-orange sweatshirt and a tan walked with a swagger across the space, ushering the nurse and his wife before him through the door of the center for genitourinary cancers.

Dr. Lawrence's face was grim. They had an excellent relationship, and he knew not to beat around the bush. Mum sat on the end of the examination bed, back straight, eyes wide to take in whatever he was about to say. He sat opposite her, and Toby and I sat side by side next to the door.

The cancer had been unaffected by the therapy. More than that, the tumors had increased in number.

Dr. Lawrence laid out her treatment options – a riskier immunotherapy drug, irradiated pellets inserted into the liver for focused radiation, or experimental therapy – and all of them sounded rotten, even though the names of the drugs were quite cute. The immunotherapy drug she had been on, Pembrolizumab, was always shortened to Pembro. The one now on offer, Ipilimumab, was referred to as Ippy. Pembro and Ippy, like good old friends from a jolly British boarding school. But Ippy was scary, with potentially powerful side-effects whose remedies could also bring side-effects.

Toby brought up how Dr. Lawrence had strongly encouraged Mum to do that first course of therapy and asked him if he felt as intent on encouraging her to try a remedy this time around. Dr. Lawrence admitted that he didn't. If he were in Mum's position, he would do it, but he knew that she had an aversion to extreme measures. She brought up again that she didn't fancy turning 80, and he countered that he had a 90-year-old father-in-law who was still kicking up his heels. But he'd understand if she said goodbye to hospitals.

His whole team was sad, and they all came in to see her, and she made them laugh. Not sad herself, she was excited at being able to drink alcohol again, and we have a great photo of her in the middle of them, everyone beaming, because she couldn't decide whether to have a gin and tonic or a rum and ginger ale.

That was a Thursday. She agreed to meet him on the Monday with her decision, and she and I returned to Linden Ponds for a strangely beautiful weekend. We floated around. We saw some of her friends and talked about the situation, we did the crossword and didn't talk about the situation, we returned some shoes (for her) and bought some clothes (for me), we walked on the beach, and we had a gentle, really nice time. Each day she said something about how she felt when she woke up, generally to do with not wanting to undergo any more treatment. On Sunday night, I said, "We're having such a nice time, and you seem so well, I need to go back to the doctor with you because it now feels unreal. Does it feel unreal to you?" She thought about that, and said, "It's not that it feels unreal, but that it doesn't matter." The sweetness of that statement, the effortless strength of that surrender, continues to ring in my ears now. She was cheerful. She was peaceful. She expressed zeal for the immediate future, and acceptance of the – what's the word for it? – not struggle – to come. She decided against treatment.

In the summer, I participated in an evening of live storytelling called "Walking in Beauty" in London, in which seven women talked about their relationships with beauty. I'd been thinking a lot about the color pink, and that became my starting point, connecting pretty quickly to my mother's favorite lip color, in another opportunity to wrangle with Mum's vivacity-mortality. What follows is what I told the crowd.

Many years ago, probably when I was in my twenties, my mother told me about how her mother had suddenly presented her with her first lipstick. "Mothers can really surprise you sometimes," she said. My mother reckons she was about fifteen at the time. She knew that her grandmother was disapproving of lipstick on girls that young, but at that time my mother was at boarding school in Sussex, her mother, my grandmother, was living in Nigeria, and my dour Scottish great-grandmother was at a safe distance in deepest, darkest Nottingham.

My grandmother, a ballet and tap dancer until her marriage, clearly felt very positively about lip color, as she famously referred to the 1960's fashion of white lipstick as looking like "worms under water." The color she may have given my teenaged mother in 1954 or '55 was Revlon's Persian Melon, as that's the color my mother remembers taking with her to finishing school in Switzerland when she was seventeen. She brought it with her as well on a trip to Cambridge ... just last month. Revlon still makes it. It is number 585, from their Moon Drops range, and it has been my mother's go-to color for roughly 63 years.

Not that she hasn't changed in all that time. But the color has changed, too. Initially more of an orange-red, described in early advertising as "A luscious golden melon with a coral flavor," it is now a bright pink. I couldn't find how Revlon describes it these days, but one blog review called it Barbie-pink. I don't know what that means either. Quite a few Amazon reviewers said they'd worn it 60 years ago and were wearing it again, one saying it was pinker than she recalled.

So, it does not represent, and has never represented, a Persian melon, but it is bright and fresh and feminine.

Feminine? Really?

A *Ladies' Home Journal* article in June 1918 said, "The generally accepted rule is pink for the boys and blue for the girls. The reason is that pink, being a more decided and stronger color, is more suitable for the boy, while blue, which is more delicate and dainty, is prettier for the girl." The preferred colors for boys and girls swapped over in the 1940s, then more unisex colors came in in the 1960s and '70s. I was born in 1966, and was dressed in pink and blue and orange and everything. My dancer grandmother knitted me a cardigan with so many colors it looked like a Missoni. And then in the 1980s, with the development of prenatal testing, people went back to pinks and blues, kitting out their nurseries with the knowledge of the gender of their unborn child.

In September 2017, my husband and I bought and moved into our first house and set about making it our own. The previous owners were a lovely family with three dogs, three guinea pigs and three daughters. Perhaps the older two had chosen the colors in their bedrooms themselves – the broad chimney breast in the middle daughter's room was covered in pink glitter wallpaper – but the infant obviously hadn't. The walls of her room were lilac. Her window blind was bright pink with white polka dots. And the pink didn't stop there. There were deep-pink feature walls in the parents' bedroom and the living room, which took five coats of white paint to obliterate. As we continued clearing the spaces for ourselves, we continued finding traces of the girls everywhere. Pink and purple hair ties around the doorknobs. Purple chalk and hair clips in the flowerbeds. Pink and purple beads in the gravel of the driveway. Once, in the bathroom, a butterfly made of pink feathers fluttered down on me from the top of the window frame. I did find a dinosaur under a bush and a giraffe in a flowerpot, but the overwhelming impression I had was of girls who were being told to be 'girly'.

And I judged that harshly.

Eventually, though, I thought about the trials of my own daughter, who had only recently begun emerging from a long, anxious funk – shall we color it blue? – during which she withdrew from friends, dropped classes, chopped off her hair, and wore neutral, baggy clothes that hid her. She wore no make-up, she wore no jewelry, she wouldn't smile for photos. If you'd asked me in the depths of that time what color I would have been most encouraged to see on her, I think I would have said pink, and red. Not blue, which for me is the least 'decided' color. I would have liked to see green, certainly – the color of life in plants. But pink or red would have shown the color of life in animals.

And I would have liked to see some lipstick. Even messy, glossy lipstick, my opinion of which was changed forever sitting in a car in Washington, DC with a male friend many years ago. We passed a woman wearing shining, wet, deep-red gloss on her plump lips, and I commented that I'd never understood why that might seem attractive because you'd obviously get the gloss all over yourself if you kissed her, and he enlightened me. "You don't imagine kissing lips like that," he said. "Oh, okay then," I said. But he continued. "You imagine them around your dick."

There are clearly traces of my dour Scottish grandmother in me, as I haven't worn gloss since.

But gloss is like sap – a sign of life, of juices flowing, and I would have welcomed such a sign on my daughter, who was covering her beauty.

On one visit to her in New York, when she was spending long stretches of the day in bed, she said to me, "I know I must look to you as if I am catatonic, but I want to reassure you that I am thinking. I am processing."

She was cocooning. Cocoons look like dead things, don't they? They don't move. Nothing's happening on the surface. But inside, an astonishing reassembling, a repurposing, a metamorphosis.

Perhaps it was the return of signs of life in my daughter that prompted my mother to give her a tube of Revlon's Persian Melon. My mother recognizes signs of life, and cheers them on. Her Persian Melon lips shout and cajole. They purse and protest. I have a photo of her from March, at the March for our Lives gun-control rally in Boston. She's standing with her handwritten "Guns are for Cowards" poster, dressed head to toe in pink winter gear. Her 90-year-old friend, Elizabeth, with her own poster, is all in red. They are like two hearts pumping.

My daughter doesn't feel the lip color suits her, but she really wishes it did. "Annie puts it on (she calls my mother Annie rather than Granny due to early-life pronunciation issues) – Annie puts it on and BAM! She feels ready. I want that." Because pink *is* such a decided color.

I want that, too, but I have put my mother's Persian Melon lipstick on and wiped it right back off many times in my life, and I can't see that it suits me either.

When she was in England last month, I watched her lips one night at dinner as they spoke engagingly with the server, and ate, and joked, and then as, around 9 o'clock, she suddenly began to look a little small. I watched her lips say, "I do get a bit tired about this time."

My mother has terminal melanoma. During her terrific visit, I had only been aware of signs of life, but on that evening she was gently revealing one of the messengers of her death.

Tomorrow, my husband and I will fly to Massachusetts for her 79th birthday. She will continue to show us signs of life, and will also continue to communicate the signs she sees of her death. Because she is completely owning this train taking her out of here. The cancer is overtaking her liver, and she has named it Lily. Anything but lily-livered, however, she is ready. She will get thinner, and yellower, and her lips will look like worms under water. I will apply Persian Melon to them when she can't.

May I be ready too.

Grapple, grapple, grapple, grapple. And cry. That was the year of tears. In a notebook Andy and I share for to-do lists and plans, there's a list I wrote titled Things Alison Needs Help With:

- *Website Locked Out page*
- *Mastercard*
- *photos*
- *office floor*
- *deciding how to get to Orkney and where to stay*
- *crying all the old cries*

It was the year of a dawn simulator to deal with seasonal affective disorder so I could survive the winter, and by early 2019, of anti-depressants.

Escitalopram
Mum and I are on the same drug
Only I know this

(APRIL 22)

For Mum, though, 2018 was an astonishingly wonderful year. After she decided to forego further therapy, Toby asked her if there was anything she regretted not having done. Within three weeks they were doing everything there was to be done at the Grand Canyon. Then she waited to feel rotten. A little nausea came and went, but the liver tumors that were predicted to start bothering her within a few months simply didn't. She had her concerns, of course, and some panic attacks, but she felt well. Very well. She traveled domestically and internationally, attending the launch of her biography of Clarence Bicknell in Cambridge, England in June, and Bicknell-related events in Italy in October. She walked and swam and wrote and danced at a wedding. Just before the New Year she wrote in her annual year-end letter to her friends:

> By June, I was still feeling pretty good, and wanted to go to England
> when my new book, Marvels: The Life of Clarence Bicknell, had
> its launch at the Fitzwilliam Museum in Cambridge. Hospice
> couldn't be responsible for me abroad, so I resigned, after my nurse
> had assured me that I could return whenever I needed to. I saw the
> doctor again in July, at which point he remarked, "Your immune
> system is performing well." At my next visit, in September, he said,
> "I am totally mystified by you." And when I saw him again in
> November, he prodded and poked around, and said, "I can't feel
> anything wrong with you." His theory now is that I have had a
> delayed reaction to the immunotherapy, something that is unusual
> but not without precedent. It's very strange to prepare for one's
> mortality, and then to get another chance at life!

She may indeed have had a delayed reaction to the immunotherapy she underwent at the beginning of 2018. Or …who knows? Nobody. The only thing we know now is that her melanoma continued to metastasize in secret. When visiting Jane in DC at Christmas, she saw technicolor flashing lights in front of one eye. She characteristically discounted them, just days before sending off that elated email. In January we learned they were seizures caused by one of three brain tumors.

CLUNK. We were back to fearing for her life.

She agreed to go on anti-seizure medicine, to give up driving immediately, and to undergo radiation to stop the growth of the tumors and possibly shrink them. She got it in her head, because the very high-powered neurosurgeon who ushered her in and out of radiology told her she should be optimistic because the focused treatment was very effective, that she might well have a meaningfully long time left to live – again. But it wasn't a huge shock to her when the treatment only bought her a few months. She had prepared for her death. After that first round of immunotherapy failed, she had decided that dramatic treatments designed to save her life could too easily wreck what was left of her life. She remained intent on taking advantage of continuing to feel quite well, and then on dying when she didn't. I am convinced that witnessing first her father's Parkinson's (and her mother's laborious care of him), then her mother's Alzheimer's and strokes, then my father's ALS, in addition to perceiving the progress of her own glaucoma and worsening balance, all contributed to her resistance to a ninth decade.

I have a very strong image of her in my mind from one of her visits to Singapore, where I lived from 1999 to 2016. It was probably 2013. She was standing with her hand on the open door of the apartment, and my impression is that she was not just going out to the library to write as she did each day on those visits, but that she was heading out to visit somewhere even more interesting, as she did from time to time. It might have been Cambodia. Just before walking out the door she said, "Well, now at least I know how I'm going to die. Melanoma. I'll take that."

And then she set about living.

THE NOTEBOOK

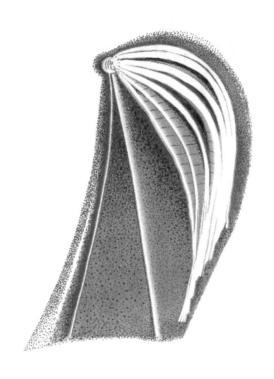

When Mum's three brain tumors (Mel, An, and Oma) finally began to assert themselves, she was in the process of trying to finish a novel she had begun in the 1980s. I remember visiting my parents in their little cottage in Maine and being awoken by the sound of her banging away at her computer in a perimenopausal frenzy. I also remember reading it there, some years later, when it was finished, and crying at the end. I thought it was great, but Mum wasn't so sure. She put it down and picked it up, put it down and picked it up over the decades, re-titling it as she went. It was *Cinchona*, then *Peter Mason*, then *Spanish Town*, and at last, *The West Indian*. In between, she wrote other books.

With the metastasis of her cancer and the failure of the immunotherapy came the desire to finalize the novel. She read it through again and pronounced it worthy. A few agents read it and pronounced it good, but couldn't commit to trying to sell it in the current market. She could see how long finding a UK fiction agent was taking me, and knew she didn't have that luxury. She decided to self-publish, and hired Bruce Kennett – book designer, photographer, author, and wonderful companion to her in various adventures – as designer.

Finalizing meant adding a few pages she'd had in mind, near the end of the book. Bruce was going to come and spend a couple of days with her in April to get the book done and uploaded onto Amazon's publishing platform. Mum liked the idea of publishing in April, on my 53rd birthday.

On my own daughter's 24th birthday, in March, Mum called me in England. "Ali," she said, "I'm so confused." She'd been unable to think clearly or write clearly since the day before, but hadn't wanted to disturb my time with Kiri. Mary Ann had had to work hard to convince her to talk to me about what was happening. Mum hadn't wanted to disturb my brother either. Normally Toby was only about 45 minutes away, but that weekend he was on an annual outdoorsy trip with friends.

She told me that a friend had visited and had told her she seemed to be exhibiting the symptoms of a mild stroke. Her mouth might be a little down on the right side, she told me, having looked in the mirror. She was definitely dragging her right foot a bit, although she heard that rather than felt it. She didn't call the hospital because she was finished with hospitals. She hadn't called her hospice provider either.

"Have you talked to The Nurses?" I asked her, meaning her friends across the hall, Sybil and Nancy, retired RNs who shared an apartment like college roommates. They and Mum often watched *Jeopardy* together, and Mum had turned Nancy on to gin. When Mum twisted her ankle stepping off a kerb, she called The Nurses to see if they thought it was broken. Not to have called them was crazy, and evidence of her confusion. I asked her to hang up, go across the hall, and tell Sybil and Nancy what was going on, then call me back.

When I talked about that phone call later, she couldn't recall going across the hall. But she did do it, and The Nurses promised to look in on her regularly.

That was Sunday. On Monday I had to talk to a creative writing class. During a break, I called Sarah, one of Mum's friends in England, who was soon to get on a plane to stay with Mum for about a week. Sarah's husband had died of metastatic melanoma several years before, and during the past months I had been talking with her daughter about what his final months were like. "He wasn't in pain," she told me. "We sat in the garden and did a butterfly count." When I reached Sarah, she had already travelled to London to be ready to head to Heathrow Airport early the next morning. She was one hundred percent willing to be whatever Mum needed her to be, and made no changes to her trip.

Then I called Toby, although Mum had told me in no uncertain terms not to.

"She didn't want me to call you," I said.

"Of course she didn't," he replied, and then imitated her: "'It's only a *stroke.*'"

(Remember, our mother was British, and grew up during the Second World War and the following years of rationing. She wasn't famous for keeping calm, but she always carried on.)

Toby was due back that evening. I told him not to scramble for an earlier flight, as The Nurses were on the case.

When he got back, he dropped his things at home and went to spend the night with Mum. Her English friend arrived the next day. A few days after that, Bruce drove down from New Hampshire to be midwife for *The West Indian*.

Mum gathered herself together. Imagine it: She couldn't write by hand, and when she typed it took too much out of her, and she could no longer spell correctly. She asked all her remaining mental faculties to gather, to huddle, to work as a team one last time, and she dictated to Bruce what remained to be written.

I arrived at Linden Ponds ten days after Mum's confused phone call. On the wide sill of the broad, living-room windows was a pile of books, a clutch of *Boston Globe* crosswords, and an A4-size graph-paper notebook, spiral-bound at the top. It was open to a page of hurried writing in pencil, in a hand I didn't recognize. When I read the words, I knew right away that it was Bruce's hand, taking down Mum's finishing touches to her novel.

"Go!" it says in the middle of the page. "Make this journey."

On the day after I arrived, Mum was waiting for a call from Dr. Lawrence. She was quite anxious before speaking with him, but he told her that her symptoms had nothing to do with high blood-pressure, that he would up her steroid dosage, and that she was probably fine being left on her own from time to time. She was reassured. "He basically gave me good news," she said, "which is that the tumors are spreading."

Mum and I used that notebook for our To Do list during the nine days we were together in her apartment before she moved to the Pat Roche Hospice Home, and I carried on using it for my own list after that.

- *Contact antiques people*
- *Dentist*
- *Donate plants – who?*

It wasn't until after she died that I turned to the front of the notebook to see what else was in there. Mum had sooooo many notebooks. If you're a writer, maybe you do as well (particularly if you grew up without electronic gadgets). Usually they only pertained to a single project. For some reason, this otherwise unremarkable one contained nuggets of several projects.

At first glance, I thought the first page had to do with *Phiz: The Man Who Drew Dickens* (Chatto & Windus, 2004), her biography of Hablot Knight Browne, Dickens' principal illustrator. That was her second book. Her first had been *Fasten Your Seat Belts: History and Heroism in the Pan Am Cabin* (Paladwr Press, 1995). Like many of the company's flight attendants and former stewardesses, Mum felt Pan Am's demise as a tragedy. That first book was her response.

Looking more carefully at the notebook's first page, I recognized that the notes there had to do with her fourth book, *Giambattista Bodoni: His Life and His World* (David R. Godine, 2015). (Her third had been a translation of the classic French coming-of-age novel by Alain-Fournier, *Le Grand Meaulnes* [Vintage Classics, 2009].)

Bodoni was a prominent 18th-century typographer, and Mum's notes are about letter punches and how to make them: "files and gravers are the most important tools," "Sit up straight, maintain your angle, be patient."

The next three pages are a list of slides my father took on Everest. After he died, during her work on Bodoni, Mum organized the slides for donation to The American Alpine Club. You can view them on their website if you search for the James T. Lester, Jr. Collection.

Then we're back to Bodoni notes ("Call the rower of royal barges," "Explain quarto octavo etc."), and then notes that look like someone had asked her to give feedback on their writing ("Slackens a bit in the middle").

And then there is the explosion of Bruce taking dictation. I can hear his pencil on the paper when I look at it.

The West Indian was her sixth book, the second of two completed after her terminal prognosis. The fifth was another biography, the absolutely lovely *Marvels: The Life of Clarence Bicknell, Botanist, Archaeologist, Artist* (Troubador, 2018).

While the novel is set in the 1700s, it draws on her memories of childhood in Jamaica. Maybe, like me, you won't find it at all surprising that she wanted to return to the island by finishing her work on *The West Indian* before she died.

It's Time to Get Out of the Water

"Don't you dare go under the surface
Pretending you can't hear my call.
It's time to get out of the water;
Not in five minutes, child, but now!
Your lips are blue and your eyes are red,
Your fingers are washerwoman wrinkled.
Child, you feel like a fish in my grip."

And at night, in my dream, again the voice says:
"You mustn't go in, in your best dress, child."
And I stand at the edge of the shimmering pool,
And I gaze at the water, and gaze
In the water, and I'm almost done in
With desire. Slyly I dip
My toe in the pool, and slip,
And throw myself in the pool, and oh
It's so lovely and so what I wanted.

ROUTINE

Less than two weeks after Mum experienced those stroke-like symptoms, she had a tour of the Pat Roche Hospice Home – hereafter referred to as PRH – and made the decision to move there the moment she walked through the front door. She'd had her eye on the place for years, passing by it on her way to walks at the top of Turkey Hill, and had imagined the relief that being there would bring. It flooded her right away.

Imagine a broad brick house with dormer windows in a gray tile roof, two porches at the back and a magnificent beech tree on the side. Before being bought by the NVNA and Hospice health agency in 2011, the house had been a wealthy family's summer residence, and became a Quaker rest home for the elderly in 1958. Mum had the idea that it was the Quakers who had introduced the hospice concept to the United States. I looked into that after she died, and she was wrong. The first hospice in the United States was founded in Connecticut in 1974 by Florence Wald, formerly the dean of the Yale School of Nursing. But the hospice philosophy certainly jibes with that of the Friends. In an article in the online *Friends Journal*, chaplain Katherine Jaramillo summarizes their approach to dying and death as discussed at a Quaker Women's Theology Conference in 2017:

> A Quaker approach would be a mindful, conscious, and prepared approach, with an excitement – or at least a willingness – to enter the mystery of death. It was agreed that a Quaker approach would involve less denial that someone is dying or that death is imminent. There is a value for listening, hearing one another's experiences, and entering new situations with curiosity, not offering answers. Especially for Liberal Friends, but for some Evangelical Friends as well, there was less focus on an afterlife.

> A Quaker approach would be a well-ordered approach, with orderly records, legal documents, and final letters and lists of wishes. Friends agreed that cremation was customary and in alignment with Quaker values.

That was Mum, to a T. More on that in "On the Nature of Things".

Mum knew she had weeks rather than days to live when she moved to residential hospice, and had made me go over the calculation of the cost several times – what if she lived one more month? Two? Three? She triple-checked with Toby and me that we were comfortable with her spending our inheritance, but she needn't have. Just as when our father died and left all his assets to Mum for her comfort, we felt that her funds should still work for her comfort. Also, her mental comfort would be served in knowing that she wouldn't be asking a great deal of us at the end. Neither of us would have minded managing a schedule of care for her between us and home hospice visits, but she wanted to take such admin off our list of responsibilities. It's possible that she also wanted, sometimes, to be alone.

On the day we moved her, Toby and I packed her things into his car. I stayed downstairs when he went back up to escort her down. He told me later that as they walked toward the door, she said a sweet little goodbye to the furniture she passed, all of it comfortable and comfortably mis-matched – the reproduction Eames chair she loved to read and nap in, the coffee table made out of a huge slice of burnt mahogany in St. Croix, the palest-pink velvet sofa whose feather cushions she plumped and stroked, her grandmother's Regency secretaire. "Goodbye. Goodbye. Goodbye." She was grateful for their years of service, but no longer needed them or the things that would weigh on her mind if she were to stay. She knew herself well, and had no interest in allowing her mind to be dragged toward niggly concerns as she was dying. She was such a project-oriented person, and when she was at home she kept being bothered by chores she hadn't done. Tiny chores. For example, she knew that there was a very old piece of cucumber in the fridge that she hadn't taken out. She lay down for a nap one day, and after some moments of quiet she suddenly piped up to tell me that wizened nub was there, and could I please dispose of it so she could sleep.

Once she had settled in at PRH, a very pleasant routine settled in as well. She had to be woken early for her medications – anti-seizure, anti-inflammation – and one of them needed to be taken with food, so they fed her early as well. Don't imagine her eating in her bed, not at first. The room had a bay window overlooking a field and woodland, part of Weir River Farm. A herd of Belted Galloway cattle grazed there, and the view also featured wild turkeys, bluebirds, woodpeckers, hummingbirds (when the weather grew warmer), a hawk, and a coyote.

She ate her huge breakfasts at a table there: blueberry pancakes, omelet, yoghurt, fruit cup, coffee. The prednisone gave her a terrific appetite, so she didn't waste away as she had thought she might when the idea was that the cancer in her liver would be what took her. Her arms and legs eventually grew very thin, but she developed 'steroid moon face', as the nurses called it, which was much less distressing, and actually quite cute. Her tummy rounded out.

Braless, pot-bellied
A Venus de Willendorf
Skinny arms and legs

(MAY 29)

They gave her a shower after breakfast, so that when I arrived in those first weeks, she was sitting up in a chair by the table, clean, dressed, lipsticked, reading something interesting on her Kindle or chatting with a friend

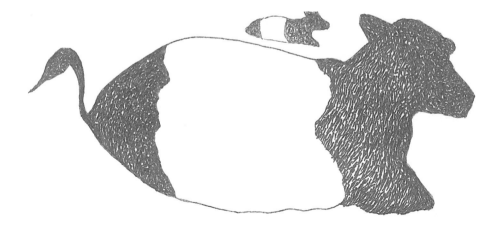

who had scheduled a visit for that morning. We found it very helpful to maintain an old-school calendar. Mum wasn't able to remember what day it was, but she knew to look at the calendar. Both she and the hospice staff could check on whether a visitor was expected. In our case, I was usually the contact person for visits, but Mum's friends would also write on it when they planned to come again, for me to see if I arrived after they had left in the morning.

We'd start our day together with her correspondence. She had tried for some days to keep writing to people herself, but neither her fingers nor her mind behaved in those moments. She could read without trouble, but I read her emails to her so that I was already in position to type the response she dictated. I made it clear to the people who had written to her that I was doing the typing, so that they knew I was also reading their emails. Mary Ann responded with "Dear Valison" early on, so I started signing off that way to Mum's close friends.

Amanuensis
No, amenuendaughter
I am now her hands
(APRIL 21)

Wind, pull, hook, wind, pull
Mum can't finish this blanket
I am now her hands
(APRIL 22)

Emails could take quite a while, as my mother had a lot of friends, and we were contacting bloggers and reviewers about *The West Indian*. She also had me write to Poland Spring ("100% NATURAL SPRING WATER. AND PROUD OF IT."). She asked me to write to them in her voice, saying that she was in hospice care and that her dying wish was that they would live up to their message of providing a 'natural' product and stop polluting the world with plastic. They replied, pretty quickly, thanking her for her feedback, and saying her message would be forwarded to the appropriate department. That was that, but she wasn't frustrated. Writing that dying wish got the subject off her mind. She'd done what she had planned to do, and what she could do, and she was happy.

We had lunch downstairs in the large room where patients and families and friends could gather or rest. There was a spacious kitchen area, with a big fridge we could keep our food in; a dining area facing double glass doors onto the lawn and the field beyond; a TV area with sofas; and a gas fireplace area with overstuffed chairs and a table for games. Nearly every day, armed with her ravenous appetite, Mum ordered a BLT with barbecue chips and a side of pickles, and ginger ale. One time, the volunteer who arrived bearing this meal on a tray stopped as she came up to the table, looked at the two of us, and said, "I thought I might have been bringing this meal down for a pregnant woman!" Mum had never been enamored of potato chips before, nor of pickles. She liked them both, but kept an eye on her salt intake, as her blood pressure was high. Now she couldn't get enough of either, and even when brought a whole cereal bowl full of chips, rather than just a handful on the side of her plate, she'd eat them all.

One of the results of the damage her brain tumors were doing was that she couldn't feel when there was food on her lips. A piece of potato chip an inch long could be sticking out of her mouth as she chewed or talked, and she'd have no idea. Before she moved to the hospice home, I would put a table mirror in front of her when we ate together, so that she could check on her face-food herself, but she actually didn't mind when my brother or I pushed the food back in for her like a parent would for a small child, so we didn't use that mirror at the Pat Roche House. She liked to look pretty, but she wasn't vain, and she let the face-food be funny.

We had simple, aimless chats, sometimes peppered with the surprise of a memory.

> "I remember this.
> The sound of my granny's teeth
> Chewing strawberries."
>
> (MAY 2)

We watched the cows, and the arrival of spring. When the weather was pleasant, after lunch we would walk, slowly, slowly, out the front door and around the side of the house to a bench in the garden, where she would lean back and tip her face to the sun. My brother was often with us at lunchtime and in the garden, and he has smiling photos – genuine smiles – of Mum on that bench with him; with me; with each of his three daughters, Emma, Kate, and Sage; and with his wife, Catherine.

I lay on the grass
And the earth was warm and strong
We will be okay

(APRIL 21)

Returning from the garden one day when Mum could still get around with a walker, we encountered a black-and-brown long-haired chihuahua on our way to the elevator. It was the sweetest, chill-est chihuahua I think I'll ever meet, and his name was Spider. We were told that he was there most Thursdays, paying visits to residents as a therapy dog. I thoroughly enjoyed giving the back of his silky neck a scratch, and when I got back up off the floor I asked Mum if she'd like to have Spider come and see her when he was around. "No," she said, and drew herself up to look down her nose. "I don't have time."

She did have time for a daily dose of chocolate. Mum had a large chest of drawers next to her bed, for clothes, and a small one opposite her bed, for whatever. In the third drawer down of the small one she had snacks for the cocktail hour, and in the bottom drawer, the chocolate stash. We took to taking out all the varieties that people had brought and laying them out on her bed after lunch. I called it the chocolate buffet. Mum started calling it the chocolate boutique one day, and I didn't correct her, and it was the chocolate boutique forever after that. We were allowed three pieces. One of her friends brought a jar of raw chocolate made into raisin-sized morsels, which had wolfberries and other nutritious ingredients in them. We decided that those were medicinal, so we could have one or two of those on top of the decadent chocolate we were allowed. We sat and we savored. Mum was so good at that.

And then it was time to brush her teeth. I didn't do that for the first few weeks. It hadn't occurred to me that it would be necessary. But Mum's breath smelled sour. We realized that she had trouble feeling when there was food inside her mouth as well as out, in between her cheek and gum. Step one was for her to use her pinky to feel around and clear as much food as she could that way. Then we'd go into her bathroom and she'd rinse her mouth out and spit into the sink, and invariably we'd exclaim at what we saw there. Then I'd brush her teeth for her. It didn't remind me of brushing my children's teeth. It's been so long since I did that, and I don't really remember what it was like. No doubt I was on autopilot a bit at those moments, getting them ready for daycare or bed. My old dog's teeth require daily brushing, and I compared it to that instead. Mum often told me how patient I was being with her, but I didn't feel like that at all. I felt lucky she wasn't trying to get away from me.

Then she would pee, which she could wipe herself, and sometimes poo, which she couldn't. I hadn't anticipated wiping her bum either. And I didn't have to do it. A nurse or an aide would have been perfectly willing to do anything I didn't want to; Mum was often the only person in her wing of the house, and there was plenty of help to be had. It wasn't so much that I wanted to wipe her bum, but rather that I wanted Mum to be comfortable, as quickly as possible. I didn't want to make her wait for me to get an aide, I didn't want her to feel a break in our flow, even if she would have completely understood it. I tried to keep her looking and feeling good, rearranging her hair to cover the bald spots that resulted from radiation, putting lipstick on her top lip so she could press her lips together and apply it herself to the bottom. Sometimes it was indeed Persian Melon that I applied. I attended to a few other simple beauty concerns as well.

Three point two five strength
Her reading specs are perfect
I pluck her face hair

(MAY 23)

The afternoons were no less structured than the mornings. Mum had goals. She asked me to bring in her files titled 'Great Letters' so she could read through them all again. I left one file at a time behind in the evening, and by the next morning or the one after, she had read them through and had weeded out the ones she no longer wanted. Eventually she realized that keeping any of them wasn't quite sensical, but she couldn't dispose of the voices of her closest friends. That would be my job.

There were poems she wanted to read aloud together, which we did at first in the two chairs by the window; later, we lay side by side in her bed.

And there was her own poetry to sort through. She had a big binder of it, but poems also turned up in various folders in her office closet and on surfaces here and there in the apartment. She didn't just want what she'd written assembled in one place; she wanted to read through it again and decide what was good and what wasn't, and beyond that, what represented a good memory and what didn't.

> *We sort her poems*
> *Class them by age and by worth*
> *Some she bins, I keep*
>
> (MAY 2)

There were duplicate copies, and various versions, some with her notes on them, some with the edits of others – in short, the collection was a slideshow of a poet's life. We tried to order them by date, but it was getting harder for her to remember what had happened when. Once we'd read through them all and had done our best to recreate the timeline, I said I'd take them away and carry on myself. "I don't know how you're going to do it," she said. "You don't have to know how," I told her. "Just know that I will."

There was one poem we had discussed at her apartment before she moved. It was dated 12/12/17 – around the time the melanoma was found to have metastasized to her liver, and was clearly part of her approach to wrangling with the diagnosis. She had told me that it was inspired by a famous poem, but I couldn't remember what she'd said, and for some reason I hadn't put that poem together with the rest of them. A couple of weeks before she died, I asked her what the inspiration had been, but she couldn't remember. She didn't seem to truly remember the poem I was referring to either. The next day I found it and brought it with me to read to her. She listened with her eyes closed, and kept them closed when I'd finished. "So?" I said, and waited for her to tell me what had inspired her to write it in this form. I had to figure that out myself later, because all she said was, "That is a very good poem."

It is.

Lucy's Bird
(After "A Nocturnal Upon St. Lucy's Day", by John Donne)

It is the winter solstice, deep midnight
Of the year. Wan hours yawn bleakly; noon
Glides low on watery sun. The moon,
Pale, idiotic moon, slurs clouded light.
The ground is frozen, wrapped
in frost, barren, unyielding, wormless, sapped.
Black fingers stab the sky, warped and cracked.
All is nothing. All is anomie.
A bird pecks a red berry from a tree.

Look at him now, you who would birders be.
Observe his stiff stick legs and ruffled feathers;
how can he sing when the weather's
freezing his song? His tweeting spree
                    is spring's sweet busyness.
Quintessence of quiet and of emptiness,
of silent syrinx, void, and nothingness,
he's lost his voice, while I have become
of winter's abstinence the sum.

All others from such absences derive
Some hope, some trust in things to come. They know
The fast will end. Fat spring will show
Fat buds, fresh sap, a world alive,
And tumbling into sin.
I roil in the remembrance of us falling in,
lying in, drowsing in, frying in, dying in
concupiscence. But what about our souls,
our dragging souls. Yes, what about our souls?

What is a soul, and what of it? A shroud,
A cloud, a something clinging, hanging on,
Lingering when our body's gone?

Does it smell? Is it endowed
With humor and with grit?
Dear friends, please tell me what you think of it.
And love, please tell me what you think of it.
Are soul and love shadows, creeping this night
So surreptitiously towards the light?

All night St. Lucy has persisted, lighting
Candle after candle to adorn her crown,
Scorching her hair. The smell! Her gown
Is dirty. She's exhausted, fighting
Sleep. Sleep wins. She sinks,
But as she sinks she hears a click, she blinks
And from the nowhere she perceives a squint
Of light. The bird's still there. He gives a squawk,
Flashes his breast, and flies away. I walk.

At 5:30 each evening, a nurse would bring in a gin and tonic with lime. Mum's gin was kept in the locked room next to the nurses' and aides' station opposite the elevator, with all the medication. All the *other* medication. The gin accompanied Mum when she moved there, and the home kept tonic water and limes stocked for her. The nurse brought a bowl along with her drink. From the 'crunchies' drawer, Mum would choose what she wanted from her favorite snacks from Trader Joe's – peanut butter-filled pretzels, multi-seed rice crackers with tamari soy sauce, and a rice cracker medley. That was often when I left her to ride the 6.5 miles back to Linden Ponds on the bike Catherine loaned me. Mum would be sitting in the chair by the window with an enjoyable evening ahead of her. Something interesting on the Kindle to read during her cocktail, followed by a light dinner of the soup Catherine had thought to buy for her, delivered by Toby each week, followed by *Jeopardy*. After that she was ready for the getting-ready-for-bed process.

Here are the books she read during her nine weeks at PRH:

The Library Book by Susan Orlean

I Am God by Giacomo Sartori

Between You & Me: Confessions of a Comma Queen by Mary Norris

The Telling Room by Michael Paterniti

Conversations with Friends by Sally Rooney

The Temptation of Forgiveness by Donna Leon

Driving Mr. Albert by Michael Paterniti

My Year of Rest and Relaxation by Ottessa Moshfegh

The Idiot by Elif Batuman (54%)

Counting Sheep by Axel Lindén

Elevation by Stephen King

The Dinosaur Artist by Paige Williams (64%)

I Contain Multitudes by Ed Yong (27%)

The Farmer's Son by John Connell

The Trial of Lizzie Borden by Cara Robertson (35% – she was enjoying it, and I'm sure she would have finished it if she could have)

Doesn't it all sound charming? It *was* charming! It was, in short, Mum's retirement. Her stepping away. Her retreat. Intact, her character wouldn't have been able to tolerate having only such pint-sized, gentle projects as reading through her diary from her time in finishing school in Switzerland, culling her contact list, and figuring out exactly how many prunes to eat at bedtime to ensure comfortable digestion the following day (two, usually). But her tumors, slowly and surely robbing her of memory and of physical strength and coordination, meant she couldn't entertain complicated thinking.

We want the story
What is this desk's provenance?
Should have asked last week

(MAY 14)

"Female cardinal?"
"Yes. . . I used to know so much."
Knowledge ebbs. And ebbs.

(MAY 19)

Plus, I mean, *PLUS*, by the time she was at PRH, she accepted her situation – not just that she would soon die, but how she was dying. When she couldn't find a word or remember a connection, she'd try as hard as she could, and then shrug and let it go. When her fingers started wiggling with minds of their own, she thought it was funny to show people. The deaths on her wing didn't perturb her at all. On the contrary. People arrived in order to be as comfortable as possible and then die when the time came, and that's what happened – to tall Mary, whose friends and hairdresser and beautiful tall daughters provided a steady stream of smiling, listening visitors; to Lebanese Al, whom the nurses called 'the king', whose small, strong, blond, Massachusetts-born wife stayed on a cot in his room and shared hummus and tabbouleh with me; to the Southeast Asian pater familias whose gathered descendants gave the ground floor a festive atmosphere; and to others I only knew as a pair of feet at the end of a bed seen through a half-open door. They were a regular reminder that while death in hospital is felt as a failure, death in hospice is a success.

JUST ONE ROOM AFTER ANOTHER

The counterpoint to my parents' downsizing dramatically as they aged was my aunt's continuing to pull things to her, piling them up around her.

I love my aunt
so I wish someone would invent
an EpiPen for proud, anemic old hoarders.
"Hello Aunt!" I'd say as she pushed me away
from the apartment door and closed it behind her,
as I took her into my arms,
not even trying to peek inside this time,
not caring how narrow the passage
between the sideboard groaning with loose change
and peppermints and heirlooms,
and the dining table creaking with catalogs
and DIY projects and sharpened pencils
had become,
because I had the solution.
Where is her flesh?
I'd need ten seconds against some flesh.
I wish someone would
invent an EpiPen for ferociously independent,
weak old ladies, which didn't require flesh
or ten seconds.
I need a Star Trek *gadget.*

I need a zapper.
"Hello Aunt!" I'd say, taking her into my arms,
and I'd zap her, psssst!
I'd say, "Oops! Static!" when she reacted.
Then we'd go to dinner,
and when I got her back home
she'd leave the door open for me
to follow her in.
We'd stand, single file,
between the sideboard and the table,
and after she took a few breaths
her beautiful, knobby hand would rise from her side
and point at her mother's silver coffee service.
She'd look back over her shoulder.
"Want that?" she'd say.

(JUNE 2018)

The counterpoint to my mother's sporadically eventful relationship with melanoma was my aunt's tumultuous relationship with...well... you name it. (I was very tempted to call this chapter 'The Shitstorm'.) By our middle years, of course, most of us already know how dramatically things can devolve. The reason I'm including some details of the litany of never-quite-life-ending catastrophes that packed out the last years of my aunt's life is rather to describe how differently we had to manage the experience with her, and the strategies that kept us sane(ish).

Jane was my father's sister, six years younger than he and six years older than my mother. She was intelligent, charming, generous, funny, warm, easy-going, curious, well-traveled and optimistic. She was selfish, proud, shy, querulous, old-fashioned, riddled with regrets and terrified of making the wrong choices. She had lived a fascinating, often bohemian sort of life, devoting nearly her entire working career to Radio Free Europe, a U.S. government-funded organization established at the beginning of the Cold War to transmit uncensored news and information to audiences behind the Iron Curtain. Her personal life included many an intense and international romantic adventure, but she bemoaned never having married and

68

had children. She'd wanted five. I've never met a bigger bundle of contradictions, and she was a wonderful seed for what for grew into my first published novel, *Lillian on Life*.

We began expecting a cataclysmic death from her over a decade before her last breath, because she was far too easily distracted and her driving had become a knuckle-whitening experience for the passenger. Also, she was anemic. Her blood didn't clot well and wounds refused to heal. She had osteoporosis, leading to compression fractures in her spine and several rounds of vertebroplasty, the injection of acrylic cement into the damaged bone. She began to curve forward, shrinking her statuesque five-foot-ten frame. And still, she continued to be one of the most beautiful women the world has ever known.

In the early winter of 2006, she fell on an icy sidewalk and shattered her femur. After hospital and rehab stays, and some months driving only a mobility scooter, she was back behind the wheel. A year after my father died, she was in a car accident that landed her in hospital. It was the beginning of a great deal of worry about her, and of communication among Mum, Toby and me. As things got more complicated, the communication included her closest friends and a care manager, and we referred to ourselves as 'Team Jane'. Jane had no children to interpret her needs to the rest of us, so Team Jane did its best. She had many doctors, doctors had many opinions, and she was an extremely unreliable narrator of her own story, so our communication with each other was paramount. I can't underline it enough: When communicating with family and friends about an emergency, be open, be clear, write things down to each other. Don't just call. You'll want to double-check the facts, I promise you.

I think that car accident compressed one of Jane's lungs. Mum flew to be with her. Toby was in France and I was in Singapore but would be arriving in the States with Andy in a week for our annual summer visit, and we would hurry to see Jane. Mum sent us this report:

Things are a bit better today. They've got the drugs right so that she's relaxed and out of pain, and yet she's responsive when roused, e.g. she can communicate if she's comfortable or not by squeezing a hand. I had a long talk with gorgeous Steve (Jane clearly enjoys being roused by him; he's such a beauty) and he said that they can't remove the breathing tube just yet because when she yanked it out yesterday, she couldn't get enough breath to speak. There's

*every reason now to hope that after two or three more days of
"healing" on the tube and because the sedation is right she will be
able to speak when the tube is removed. She will start receiving
some food through the tube later today.*

That was another long haul, but haul Jane did. She never drove again,
though. She talked about getting a new car, but this was the one time
where we celebrated her difficulty with decision-making.

Later, she was discovered to have myelodysplastic syndrome, in which
the bone marrow fails to produce enough robust cells to promote healing.
This helped to explain both her healing issues after relatively simple sur-
geries like a bunionectomy, and her anemia, which required infusions of
a drug called Procrit twice a week. It also meant that surgeons prevari-
cated every time she asked for knee replacements to alleviate the intense,
audible, bone-on-bone pain of daily life.

And then, in March of 2016, another report from Mum:

*It's been a tough week for Jane. When I talked to her on Monday
after her session at Sibley, she told me they were worried because
her blood pressure was so low (90/40) and that she should see
her doctor. So she saw Carol Horn on Tuesday, who took her off a
diuretic she had been taking for swollen ankles (not that they were
swollen, but they had apparently been at some point). Carol told
her to be in touch after her Thursday visit to the hospital. Yesterday
at Sibley, they were even more alarmed about her blood pressure
and carted her off to the Emergency Room, where they diagnosed
a significant heart murmur. The docs then mutter-muttered about
putting in a pacemaker right away, but decided against it because
she was too compromised, but today they have decided that she
really needs one, so she will have this done on Monday morning. In
the meantime, she has had a blood transfusion and is feeling more
chipper.*

An ultrasound image of her heart led to the decision to insert a catheter to remove fluid from around it. Then she had a pacemaker inserted,
during which the surgeon nicked her lung and punctured her heart. She
made it into rehab and was getting back on her feet, but then she went
into septic shock, and Toby was called in the night to ask his permission,

as Jane's medical proxy, to put a line into a vein in her neck for the administration of drugs. She was saved.

It was not surprisingly during this very long period of hospitalization, in and out of rehab, in and out of the ICU, that Jane's fear of death emerged, and her profound panic acted as a counterpoint to the equanimity her brother had exhibited in the face of the end. Her fear led at one point to an attack during which she looked like she was staring, frozen, into the headlights of an oncoming car, unable talk to my mother about the terror. A nurse came in and demanded to know what she was so upset about. Eventually she found some words. "I don't know," she said, "when I am going to have my next vanilla milkshake."

In April, I wrote an email to Mum and Toby that I will include here in full, in case you find yourself by a bedside in need of the same sort of guidance I received.

> I just had a wonderful conversation over breakfast with a friend I haven't seen in several years. During it, I learned more about her and her experience as a psychologist in hospitals, so I talked about Jane, and her panic, and how we might help.
>
> After she listened to me, she said that since Jane is naturally in fight mode, it makes good sense to help support her sense that this can work. Trying to get her to accept her mortality sounds a bit too much like encouraging her to die, so saying what she wants to hear will help keep her spirits up. The longer she lies in bed, the more her muscles atrophy, the easier it is for her to be anxious and depressed, so if she can get out of ICU and back into a situation where she can start standing up and moving around a bit, that is best. As at this point she is making baby forward steps, it doesn't sound to my friend like it's time to try and get Jane to embrace mortality like a lover. It's not clear that she'll die very soon, so there's no point in trying to help her accept when she's in fight mode. Fight mode will help her.
>
> So, when she panics, it's good to try and keep her in the present. Take her hand, get her to look you in the eye, breathe. Distract her with chat so that her parasympathetic nervous system can stay engaged and manage her sense of well-being. Get her to tell stories.

I asked about whether it made sense to see if Dr. Dyer [Jane's long-time therapist] could come in, or at least call Jane, to talk with her about the anxiety and how to stay mentally healthy in hospital. She thought this made more sense than some sort of spiritual person, as I do, since bringing in someone spiritual might have the same effect as my flying over. If it's Dr. Dyer helping her, it's the usual coping mechanism in place, and would probably help more with the panicking.

If Jane sees that the end is near (and it may not be near – we don't know) – so, IF Jane eventually sees that the end is near, THEN it is time to help her embrace it, exhale into it, and say goodbye to us. I don't think it's that time yet, and clearly the doctors aren't ready to say that yet either. Many of the things she is suffering from can be managed and/or remedied. I do feel that it's unlikely that she will ever be well again, but it does sound like she can be better than she is now, and succeeding in that will mean staying positive. To help her, I think we need to say things that sound positive to HER, rather than to us. "When you're back on your feet," "Don't worry, there are lots of vanilla milkshakes in your future," etc. It could be true, so we need to sound as if we believe it so that she can relax and stay positive.

I hope this is as helpful to you as it was to me.

Jane was rife with infection. I did eventually fly over, and by the time I arrived to spend five days as her advocate in hospital, we had learned she had an E. coli UTI and cellulitis in her leg. Then I discovered that she had also arrived on the ward with pneumonia in both lungs, and one of them needed draining. She was in her early eighties, and she looked about a hundred. She was able to converse well, though, and was back to being withering, referring to the uncharismatic hospitalist as 'The Zombie'. She had the bed by the window; in the other half of the room, behind a blue curtain, lay a dying woman. One day a team came in to talk to this woman and her daughter about hospice care, and Jane made me be quiet so she could listen as well, but she didn't want to talk to them herself, and she didn't want to talk to me about them either.

Nobody was paying attention to her pacemaker staples, so I insisted that someone come in and have a look, as it had been a month since the operation. The incision had healed, and the staples were removed. I don't know what things are like in fully staffed hospitals, as I've only had experience with understaffed ones, but I spent a lot of time running along the hallways finding people for Jane, confirming things that seemed to have been contradicted, following up when questions weren't answered, tracking down food that had been promised. People confined to hospital rooms need an extra set of healthy legs.

She still hadn't returned home when May rolled around. Her infected legs continued to dog her. Mum wrote: "I talked to Jane last night and was so sorry to hear about the leg flare-up. Poor darling; of course she's worried. But it didn't stop her telling me about her adventures in getting a cucumber salad out of the kitchen staff. It did not meet her standards!"

Toby went to DC at the end of the month. His report to Team Jane was a typical story of horror and humor:

> I'm still in DC with Jane. After her procedure two nights ago, she
> bled more than the doctors were comfortable with, so they gave
> her another transfusion (as they'd done after the first debridement)
> and transferred her to the ICU for monitoring. Her situation wasn't
> dire, but she's weak enough that they figured they'd rather keep an
> eye on her there while she recuperated. When I left last night, they
> felt she'd be ready to transfer to a regular hospital room today. Not
> surprisingly, given that she hadn't eaten before the surgery, had
> had a general anesthetic, and was on pain medication, she was very
> sleepy and a little confused about what room she was in, but we
> had a good time nonetheless: I read her an Atlantic article about
> the psychology of Donald Trump, which got her a bit riled up,
> and I showed her a video of a moose that, bizarrely, was on the
> loose in Belmont, the Massachusetts town where I live. She threw
> her head back and cackled at that story. Later, I told her this
> whole saga she's been living is "just one room after another," to
> which she giggled and said, "That would be a good book title.
> Not A Room of One's Own, but Just One Room After Another."

On and on and on it went. Eventually she made it home, with shifts of care, 24/7 – people who mostly watched TV and fed her hot dogs from the Seven-Eleven on the corner. She told me when I called her once that she had woken up in the night to find one of them at the end of her bed with her hands on Jane's feet. When Jane asked what she was doing, the woman said she was praying for her. Jane found that both creepy and nice. I found it irritating that she'd been woken up, when surely someone can pray for you without the laying on of hands. When Mum visited, Jane was as white as a ghost. Again, we prepared for her to leave us, but then, amazingly, she agreed to move to assisted living, and started getting better, in large part I believe because the food nourished her (even though she complained about it all the time).

And then she collapsed.

The culprit this time was aortic stenosis. I remember a moment in the hospital when one of the consultants had a word with me outside Jane's room, about how at one point Jane had been unresponsive when she had come to check in on her, and they had tried various gentle means to wake her, before the strong measure of rubbing her breastbone hard with a knuckle until it pained her into consciousness. Hmmm. Well, it was a hospital, and that's the approach. They have to find out just how you are, and try and get you back out of there. Had they not been able to rouse Jane, that would I suppose have meant she was in a coma, and the consultant and I would have been having a very different conversation. Many times, I wished that Jane had been allowed to remain unconscious for longer. Perhaps she would have slipped away. But she wasn't signed on to hospice then, and we had to roll with whatever was being done.

After various tests including a balloon angioplasty to see how her aortic valve responded, the doctors didn't deem Jane a good candidate for a valve replacement. She was obviously as strong as an ox in myriad ways, and stubborn as a mule, but in this regard she was too fragile and unlikely to respond well.

When she returned to her assisted living apartment, she was on full-time supplemental oxygen, and no longer had enough strength to walk. She had taken the advice of the palliative care doctor before leaving the hospital and had signed on with a hospice care provider, but immediately took against them, and demanded to be able to see a doctor of her own as well. Her terrific care manager, Amy Silver, whom she blamed for forcing her to sign up for hospice (I was there; that's not at all what happened) organized and facilitated her appointments with the various doctors Jane needed to see, and with the others she insisted on seeing. Amy wrote to Toby about the results of those visits, as well as her own visits to spend time with Jane. Toby forwarded those emails to Mum and me, and we could ask her questions and send her our own reports. We could also vent – about hospital communication, about the state of Jane's toenails, about how piles of paper rose like trembling islands from the sea around wherever Jane was sitting.

In August of 2018, I wrote to Toby and Mum after a report from Amy about the frustrations of trying to understand the many hands not talking to each other in the hospital: "Does she, or doesn't she, have aortic stenosis? Are these panic attacks, or heart valve issues? Was it pneumonia all along? Was that doctor who said go straight to hospice a total, total dick?" A year later, when I had arrived for a visit, two weeks before Jane died as it turned out, I wrote in my own report to Toby:

> I didn't get to Jane until around 11:30. She was in the bathroom with the door open, dressed, exhausted by the task ahead. I went and got a cup of coffee. Still there when I got back. Said the moment had passed. So, off we went to The Table. Stories about The Night. The Aide. The Nasal Spray. Lunch arrived. The clear area on The Table is now so small that things need to be rearranged constantly to accommodate The Tray.

> During the day, I showed her photos. She asked me if we'd ever been through the box of photos under the table on the far side of the sofa, and we hadn't. It nearly fell apart when I picked it up, but I got it over to the other side of the room, and gave her one group of pics to look at, while I sorted out putting the photos from the exhausted box into something else. I suggested maybe the big shopping bag to the left of my chair could be divested of its old newspapers. "No, no, no! Not now! We can't do that now!" Bless her desperate heart.

> Jane went back to looking at the batch of photos, which she had started putting into piles. She had to look at the piles again to see what she had intended by them, and couldn't figure it out, and tried again, and forgot again. She was just moving them around. So I told her it was time for a rest, and helped her onto the bed, getting a whopping whiff of her panty pad. We are just this side of needing a lot more help for her, I'd say. She 'can' get herself on and off the toilet and commode, and she 'can' get herself onto the bed (although I don't think she could have easily gotten her feet up there

75

without me), but the effort is extreme, and will at some point overtax her. She said that she was nearly blacking out this morning, before I got there, just sitting at the table. Maybe getting washed and dressed had been hard.

I talked with her about getting herself all worked up, and how it challenges her heart. She gets so upset with herself when her hands shake and she can't remember things. I suggested she be kinder to herself, respecting that her body was doing its very best, perhaps saying, "Okay, hands, I'll give you a moment," rather than, "Oh stop it!!" But she's always hated her body, so that's not going to be easy.

She didn't take Ativan last night. During the day I suggested that she do take some while I'm here, so I can see the effect – she can have a witness she trusts – but I didn't remind her of that when I left. She'd had enough. So had I.

One of the many powerful-to-the-point-of-staggering memories I have of that final visit is of Jane brushing her teeth. A dental appointment within the last few months had revealed the extent of ruin in her mouth. She'd told us on the phone about how much it would cost to fix, and that she'd have to think hard about that. The second or third time she talked about it to me, while my mind was thinking "What would be the value of that at this point?", my mouth said, "Are you in pain?" She said she wasn't, so I suggested she might not bother. She didn't talk about it again.

When I visited, it was clear that brushing her teeth didn't spring to mind during the day, so I asked her if she'd like to. Her positive response looked like that of a woman lost in the desert being offered a drink of water. Her mouth must have felt very dank. We got her organized in the bathroom, and I offered to do it for her, but she turned me down, so I stood next to her as she held a blue, kidney-shaped plastic bowl under her chin and scrubbed away at her choppers. The effort was so great she did it with her eyes closed, internally focused, apparently unaware of her constant moaning.

On one of the side tables out in the living room was a photo of her brushing my hair in a shaft of English sunlight when I was seven or eight. She loved that photo of her taking care of me, and although 45 years later

I now towered over her, she would not allow our roles to be reversed. It was much, much easier to brush my mother's teeth than it was to watch Jane brush her own.

Jane hated Team Jane. She loved us all individually, but hated the thought that we talked about her behind her back. She didn't see the need for it, and I'm sorry that knowing about it embarrassed her, but it didn't stop us. Nor should it have. Her state was so variable over the years, and Mum, Toby and I couldn't be there very often. It helped us greatly when not only her care manager wrote to us but also any friend who visited typed out a report to the team. Along with our own conversations with Jane, emails from the team helped us decide when to visit and what to bring. There were times when Jane was able to drink red wine as usual, and times when she was not. There was a type of cookie she was addicted to, a type of orange she preferred. We let each other know what she was up for, and how much of it. When she was in the hospital, friends who planned to visit her would write to the group so that there would be no crowds. While the constant struggling Jane did in the last years of her life felt to me to be of dubious value, I am always consoled that during those years she can have been in no doubt at all about how much her friends and family loved her.

I hope they felt how much she loved them, but she had trouble saying it. She had been very impressed by what my father had written before he died, and wanted to be as eloquent. The problem was, and had always been, that she wanted to be perfect so much that she couldn't get started. Both Amy and I went through experiences where Jane had wanted to give a friend a card, and we had gone out and bought one for her, but then Jane had refused to write it in front of us. We knew that if we left, the card would never be written, but she gave us no choice.

Jane and I talked about how she might succeed in getting a message written to her friends. I suggested I take dictation since she was uncomfortable putting words on paper herself. Her response was to tell me stories from decades before about how terrified she was of speaking in public, as if in taking dictation I would be an entire audience sitting in judgment. Eventually I said to her, "Why don't you just send them something that says exactly what you said to me, that you love them and that they are very important to you?" "Yeah yeah, blah blah blah," she said. A simple, true message wasn't going to be good enough, for her. I know her friends, though. They would have been deeply touched by a card or email like that.

My mother and Jane frequently talked on the phone throughout their relationship, and after my father died it increased to almost daily, except when Mum was traveling. Even then, she used Skype to keep in touch with Jane, hating the idea that Jane was so often alone. She'd usually call at the cocktail hour, a nice time to revisit the day. When Mum was at PRH and her hands were becoming less and less reliable, she would use Siri on her iPhone to make the call, and would put Jane on the speaker because she had trouble holding the phone next to her ear. As a result, if Toby or I were there at the time of the call, we could participate in conversational gems like this one, which I recorded:

VAL:	Um, how are you doing?
JANE:	Uh . . . hahaha.
VAL:	Hnh-hnh.
JANE:	I guess, same as you.
VAL:	Right, right. Heh heh hnh hnh.
JANE:	It's just same old, same old.
VAL:	Yeah. Yeah. Um...
JANE:	It's a little discouraging. Are you doing any reading? Are you able to read?
VAL:	Yes, I am. I can read, and I'm reading two books, um, one is *The Trial of Lizzie Borden*, which is very interesting.
JANE:	*The Trial of Lizzie Borden*?
VAL:	Yeah!
JANE:	Who took an ax?
VAL:	Yeah! Ha ha ha ha ha ha. And she gave her father forty whacks.

JANE:	Do you remember, do you remember James, uh, wait a minute. Oh my god, what was his name? The guy I lived with for . . . James . . . James . . . Oh come on, Jane!
ALISON:	Chace!
VAL:	Chace! Chace! Chace!
JANE:	Good heavens. He lived . . . He lived in . . . We went up there every summer with the two little girls.
VAL:	Right. Right. Right.
JANE:	Oh . . . What . . .
VAL:	James CHACE.
JANE:	Chace! Yes, that's it. He lived there, and his mother was in an institution there, and we went to see her one time, and the girls came away singing, Lizzie Borden took an ax.
VAL:	Right.
JANE:	Killed her father, uh, gave her father forty whacks, or something, huh huh huh huh huh huh.
VAL:	Right. Huh huh huh huh. Oh dear.
JANE:	Gosh, I'd forgotten James. How could I do that?
VAL:	Well, easy.
JANE:	Yes, I guess you're right.
VAL:	Uh, well . . . uh . . . What more is there to say?

I imagine some people would feel sad, or even haunted, hearing their loved one's voice again after they have passed on, but it's amazing how quickly one's memory of a sequence of events can get tangled. When I think back on the three months I spent in Hingham when Mum was dying, my mind doesn't present that length of time to me at all. It feels more like three weeks. It's only when I return to the way the experience was marked in emails, photos and voice recordings that I can bring back all the threads woven in.

MUM: I'm going to be seventy-nine?

ME: No, you're going to be eighty, Mummy. In July.

MUM: I never wanted to be eighty.

ME: Well, try harder.

MUM: [laughs]

ME: Nineteen thirty-nine.

MUM: That's right. . . I never wanted to be eighty.

ME: Don't like it, do you?

MUM: Nah. . . . Got my wish.

(MAY 14)

A few weeks before Mum died, Jane called her early in the morning, sounding desperate, and told her, "I don't want to live a minute after you go." Ever the Pollyanna, Mum took that to mean that Jane had actually started feeling willing to submit to the situation. "Let's do this together," Mum told her. I got a bit nervous and called Toby. "What are we going to do?" I asked him. "You go right, I'll go left," he replied, with a smile in his voice, then said, "It's not going to happen."

He was right, of course. Jane had lost a lot of things – the love of her life, her cherished only sibling, the ability to stand and to walk, to wash herself, to read and hear with ease, to retrieve some memories both recent and decades-old. But she hadn't given these things up; they'd been taken from her. Offered the choice, she *hoarded*. If she couldn't let go of an old newspaper, how was she going to let go of her life?

On the third afternoon of my last trip to see her, I wrote to Toby:

When I got to her today, I thought she was going to die.

And at 12:45, we had brunch.

Jane had a core of steel. Her arms were mere skin on bone, but her large hands could grip you like a vise. So could her will. No matter how she felt, if there was a caller coming for brunch – particularly a gentleman caller, as there was on this occasion – she'd bloody well heave herself from her bed into her chair, get her earrings on, and rally. She'd order a mimosa and complain, as she did at every brunch, that there was no more than a thimbleful of champagne in it, and she'd converse until her oxygen tank ran low and she had trouble catching her breath.

A week after that brunch, four days after I got back to my home in England, Toby called to say that Jane had died. It hadn't, despite all our fears, been cataclysmic. Doris, an aide who had known Jane since she arrived there, and who was fond of her, found Jane sitting on the edge of her bed unable to muster the strength to proceed further into the day. Doris suggested that she lie back down instead of getting up, and Jane agreed. Doris held Jane's hand. I wonder if she had done that before. It's not my impression that she had, and it feels more to me like she intuited a change in the old girl. Jane took a deep breath and let out a sigh.

And that was the end.

When both my mother and my aunt were alive, and Mum was relaxing and enjoying her last weeks while Jane was bellyaching through her own, making her life and everyone else's more complicated rather than less so, I often felt sick with the thought that only Mum took charge of how she wanted to die, while Jane denied that she herself was dying. I had spent hours and hours of my life wishing that Jane could find it in herself to let go of the past and let go of the clutter and, in the final months, let go of the idea that the painful edema in her legs was due to anything but her compromised heart. She neared her end without an ounce of serenity, and that distressed us all.

Within a few hours of getting that phone call from Toby, however, I was surprised to find that I suddenly didn't feel Jane's final chapter was a tragedy. On the contrary. Weirdly, my heart was applauding her, even as I cried. What a woman! What women! I took my hat off to them both. They steadfastly approached their lives and their deaths in their very particular ways, and that's a form of dignity, isn't it? Jane detested dying, but even so, she stayed in the driver's seat. She was a terrible driver, but it was her life to handle. I finally relaxed into the position that it was not my place to say what they could or should have done differently, only what we, the people who loved them, might have.

In Jane's case, I wish I'd focused less of my attention on her struggle for breath and more on managing my own. I was in pain because she was in denial, maintaining that no one knew how to medicate her correctly and insisting on buying new file folders to organize her bits of paper rather than getting rid of those bits of paper. Instead of trying to help her get organized – an utter impossibility, even though she desired it so greatly – I wish I'd just taken deep breaths and released them slowly. I wish that I'd done more nodding. Inhale, nod, exhale, nod, inhale deeeeeply while nodding, exhale long and slow, with a smile, to accept that she wouldn't refer to the sheet made for her about the drugs she was supposed to be given; she'd lose it instead. To accept that she'd never even open the plastic packaging around the file folders. To waste no time wishing she could have been otherwise. She couldn't. We both would have benefited greatly if I had listened to her complaints for a bit, then tuned out, listened, tuned out, and if I had more often asked her to tell me her favorite stories from the good old days, because it sometimes happened that on the hundredth time around, I learned something new. I tried to manage my anxiety by nudging or pressing her to behave differently, which I know is a very natural, human response. It didn't help one bit, though. Not one bit.

POND LIFE

Back to Hingham.

I lived in my mother's apartment at Linden Ponds for nearly three months. I hadn't known I'd be there that long, and had bought a ticket to stay a week, but had spent the big bucks for a flexible one. I changed it three times as the situation developed, and never paid an extra cent. If you can afford to do this, I'd say do it, even if it feels like a stretch. The reduction in stress is invaluable.

My life at Linden Ponds was terrific. I slept in the dip my mother's body had made in her side of the mattress, I read her books, I tried on her earrings.

> Today, I woke drab
> And used Mum's curling iron
> It smelled like high school
>
> (APRIL 21)

In the week between our visit to PRH and her move there, Mum and I went through all her clothes, setting aside things to take to PRH, things for me, things for her grandchildren and friends, things for charity donation, things for the trash. We did the same with her jewelry and her toiletries. As I said, she didn't want to bring much with her, as this was her retirement from things as well as from activity, and she didn't want Toby and me to have more decisions to make about her possessions than necessary.

In fact, the very day after she moved to PRH, she had us spring her and bring her back to her apartment one more time, to see if, after a night away, she felt there was something she needed or wanted, and also to go through a couple of boxes of memorabilia. We learned new things: She'd won a Poetry Society bronze medal for recitation in 1954, a silver in 1955, a gold in 1956. We found the notebook where she'd written out the poem she was preparing to recite in 1956. We found a collection of telegrams my parents received on their wedding day, which included one that made her flinch. "That man almost molested me," she said, meaning he bloody well did.

When she tired, we brought her back to PRH. Thereafter, I brought the remaining boxes of memorabilia for her to peruse there. There was nothing else she wanted from her apartment.

So, I lived among her furniture, looked at the art on her walls. Toby came for a night a week, to get an early start on working together, sorting through Mum's papers and books, before visiting her at lunchtime. He came again on the weekends, often with family. He and I hadn't often been alone with each other in the past decades, what with having partners and children and parents and in-laws, and the opportunity not just to reminisce but also to learn more about each other was very warming and solidifying. In all the places we had to go together to deal with the situation – the Pat Roche House, the funeral home, the lawyer – people remarked on how fortunate we were (and *they* were) that we got along and were of one mind. They all had stories of siblings not being able to go to such meetings together or to visit their dying parent together. We know that it meant so much to our mother to see us happy in each other's company. What a crying shame it is that we were such a surprise to people. The day we moved Mum to PRH and got her settled in her lovely second-floor room, Toby went down the hall to ask the nursing aide something, and she just came right out and said, "Why are you all smiling? Why are you so happy? This is not usual!"

Mum asked me if living at Linden Ponds among so many people shuffling along with walkers depressed me at all, and I told her I felt the opposite. It was, and remains, an inspiration to me, how active the residents were, and how cheerful. I'd known it was an uplifting place to spend time, though, because of being there when Dad was dying. It reminded me a bit of college. Dinner started early, and when it was done, residents socialized at the mailboxes near the dining hall on their way back to their apartments. Sure, there was a magnifying glass hanging on a hook by the message board, and valet parking for the walkers at the dining hall, but people also had to think about whether they could fit in a bit of French conversation before yoga or aqua aerobics. They stuck their favorite photos and inspirational quotes on their doors. They developed crushes.

I hung out a lot with Mum's friends, basking in their reflected love for her. They drove me to PRH, or loaned me a car. Once I had Catherine's bicycle I could ride there, but when the weather was bad, there'd always be a knock on the door from Sybil to see if I'd prefer a dry ride over. Every week I had at least one invitation to join a couple or a group in the dining hall, and I regularly found a card or little gift for me to bring to Mum on the shelf outside her door.

Having the use of Catherine's bicycle was fantastic. I didn't need to rush over to PRH in the morning and could enjoy the roughly 40-minute, hilly ride after a leisurely breakfast. Linden Ponds residents didn't begrudge me my ability to cycle, and often I'd be sent off with a raised arm and "Go get 'em!" or similar exhortation by someone on their morning constitutional. PRH is two-thirds of the way up Turkey Hill, and I'd always arrive flushed with endorphins from the last thigh-burning push up the slope. As you can imagine, this went a long way towards addressing the slack around my knees. I think it also helped me avoid the panicky period I experienced after my father died, during which I felt like I was also going to die soon and should hurry up and GET THINGS DONE. I couldn't shake that feeling and sought the advice of a therapist in Singapore. She was able to calm me, telling me that it did make sense to feel that way, as my father's death was the first step towards my being in the oldest generation of the family. Sometimes finding out that your feelings make sense is all it takes. And sometimes those feelings find their way into a novel you're working on:

> The further south she went, the brighter the shrubbery, the
> more velvety the fields. Su wondered if her father would die. She
> wondered if he would mind dying in Cornwall. She wondered
> if he would mind dying. Would he be in good enough shape
> to consider the question? She realised she had imagined her
> parents living for ever, pursuing their projects and finishing all
> of them. Now that her avid walker of a father had been knocked
> down – by his own body – she heard the march of time. People

walked and walked and walked, tumbled like lemmings into the
sea. They were sharp for their time, and then dull, and then fell
to the sea floor like teeth moving forward in rows in the mouth of
a shark.

Maybe I didn't experience that sense of panic after Mum died because
I wrestled with those emotions in 2010, but I think it's more likely that
exercising and feeling my muscles respond, as well as being the spring
chicken in a senior community, played a big role.

The rides to Turkey Hill and back gave me time for observing and
processing, neither of which took place on the 15-minute car rides. My
thoughts settled into seventeen syllables.

Storm over, I bike.
The creeks gush. I taste iron
Crossing over them.

(APRIL 23)

The weather's warmer
Biking, I breathe open-mouthed
Little bugs crash in

(MAY 2)

Dead squirrel, dead snake
Dead box of Kentucky Fried
My mum's still alive

(MAY 11)

I ride the long hill
What comes before is easy
The short one, I walk

(MAY 14)

I came before buds
Now the cherry trees release
Pink pointillist ponds

(MAY 19)

Dead frog and dead wing
White blossoms like fresh popcorn
Eternal stone walls

(MAY 20)

Memorial Day
Old Glory and wild turkeys
Low sun through wattles

(MAY 28)

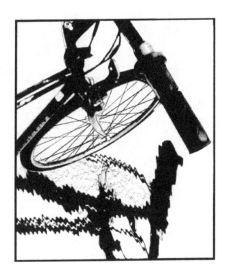

Dead cigarette pack
Dead pinecone, dead Budweiser
Mum needs more unguents

(MAY 28)

Elijah, Aram
Old names, old clapboard houses
Abner, Caleb, Seth

(MAY 28)

Dead sock, dead racoon
Dead nips, so many dead nips
Spray-painted: DEAD DRAIN

(JUNE 3)

Back in Linden Ponds in the evenings, I usually spent my time alone…

> *In bed, after ten*
> *A pair of geese flies over*
> *The freezer spits ice*
>
> (APRIL 30)

> *Bike back, six-plus miles*
> *Glass of ouzo, nuts, shower*
> *Dumb TV, laundry*
>
> (MAY 2)

Sometimes I had dinner with Sybil and Nancy, always hurrying back to their apartment in time for *Jeopardy* at their place. James Holzhauer was in the middle of his winning streak, on his way to becoming the fourth-highest-earning American game-show contestant of all time. I also had dinners with the woman who had let me pick flowers from her plot for my bridal bouquet nine years before. She was now 90, and didn't recommend the age. Compact, with immaculate salt-and-pepper hair, and walking with a pair of hiking sticks, she looked more like a retired expedition guide than a retired scientist-turned-real-estate-agent, but was full of cancer, and there were weeks when she barely ate at all. I also ate with another of my mother's friends, thin as a penny whistle, who had recently recovered from being hit by a car that had clearly been doing more than the 15mph limit within Linden Ponds. She was back to daily walks, happy to be on her feet again. She hoped to live to 90, and beyond.

Mum had younger friends at Linden Ponds, in particular Audrey and Mike, who were news junkies, world travelers, former DC lawyers pursuing their avocations of weaving and photography. I spent a lot of time at their place, drinking their rosé and their coffee. I asked Audrey in an email why they chose to move to Linden Ponds a bit earlier than most of the residents had. She wrote back, "I had worked for years on public policy that supports 'aging in place'. While I still believe that society should do things to support independence, I did not think that was really going to happen in our lifetime so a continuing care retirement community seemed like a good 'retirement' option."

If you move to a retirement community as a relatively young, healthy, friendly resident, though, you need to accept that you will likely lose a good number of the friends you make there. It was difficult to see Audrey cry over Mum's situation, despite it being evidence of love. She had never imagined that my mother would be the first of the gang to go. No one had. But since Mum was the first, and since she was going willingly, the shock and sadness of her friends was coupled with admiration, and even fascination. When people stopped me in the hall to ask how Mum was doing, they'd frequently say they were taking notes on her approach. This gave me the idea to talk to the director of Linden Ponds TV. Oh yes, TV. In a community that large, there are plenty of interesting and interested people to provide regular content for a channel. I offered to talk about my parents' choices, however they saw fit to record it, and I was introduced to Lo Steele. While all the people I met at Linden Ponds were engaged in pursuing their interests, Lo took the title of Most Engaged. She directed the musicals (most recently *Guys and Dolls*), conducted the choir, and produced numerous TV shows. Her current project, a series called *The Journey*, was focused on end-of-life decisions.

In the interview, we covered a lot of the things I've already talked about here, but the conversation led to a discussion of jealousy as well. I'm not sure that comes up very often in talk of dying, but it does occur around the dying. For example, I told Lo about how my father had had aides who came to my parents' apartment to wash him, and how much he loved their visits, giving these women his biggest smiles. And how they loved him right back. It wasn't just the aides who loved him, either. Mum once opened the freezer to show me how many pies were stacked up for Dad inside. He had trouble chewing, swallowing and digesting, but a little old bird named Ethel had discovered he liked Key lime pies, and set to making them for him with a vengeance.

When Mum showed me those pies, I thought that in her place I'd have had a word with Ethel about the inconvenient pace of her pie-making. Soon, though, I realized that Mum took it very seriously that she was in the retirement home for Dad's comfort, and this extended not only to learning how to drive an awkward van and to swallowing the easy-to-digest dining hall food into her own healthy tummy, but also to maintaining Dad's image with the ladies. He'd had to stop playing the trombone and the piano, something he'd still been doing for money only a couple of years before, and he could barely walk. Why rob him of the impression he made on women? If someone wanted to think he could eat a Key lime pie a day, Mum would let her.

There's also the jealousy of the loved one's attention, when they begin to detach from the world around them. Lo talked about how she hadn't known about the detachment process, and said, "When it happened, of course I felt, 'Oh dear, what have I done?' But it was not about me at all. He did not want to leave me. I knew that…But the moment came. And if I had been able to say to myself, 'He now needs to detach,' that would have helped."

Lo and I also talked about jealousy that can be experienced by the friends of the dying, when the family begins to circle the wagons. When Toby and I had to shift from scheduling Mum's friends' visits to protecting Mum's peace, only allowing people to come up to the room if Mum was already awake, only allowing them to stay for mere minutes, I knew how hard it was for her friends to be kept away. I remembered feeling shut out some years before by the gatekeeper of a friend who was dying of breast cancer. I couldn't understand why I couldn't visit, and I took against the gate-keeper. Stepping into that role myself, I had a sudden epiphany: "Oh! I get it! It's not about how much Mum loves anybody. Even her closest friends have to keep it so short." Love surged in a cold corner of my heart. I had to live through the situation myself to experience the relief of understanding.

THE NATURE OF THINGS

One day when Mum and I were leaving my apartment in Singapore, I went through my usual "One, two, three," which reminded me to bring my phone, my wallet, and my keys. On the way down in the elevator, she said, "Hanky, penny, prayer book, gloves," taking on the look and sound of an obedient student. She told me this was the way she and her fellow students remembered the things they were supposed to bring to church, at boarding school. My godmother, whom my mother met there, recently told me that the girls were supposed to put the penny in their coat pocket, but would often put the penny in their hanky, forget they'd done so, and pull the hanky out, sending the penny "rolling down the aisle to a clatter."

I don't know what was done about church when Mum lived in Jamaica. Not much, I expect. Perhaps she attended with her parents, but it wasn't talked about in my recollection, by any of them. I never heard her parents talk about their faith. Like all the students at Trevelyan, Mum was expected to attend, and was confirmed. So, she was brought up in the usual Church of England tradition. My father's parents were Methodists, from Missouri, but again, I never heard them talk about religion, or refer to any higher beings, for any reason. My father was expected to go to church, but not pressed on the subject once he had left home.

Dad was always an atheist. When Toby was six, in first grade, my mother was called to the school because he had announced that he didn't believe in God, even though we went to Sunday school. Mum had us go through the confirmation process as teenagers in Massachusetts in our local Episcopal church (the closest tradition to the Church of England), but only I came out of it a believer. So Mum and I went to church, where I sang in the choir (how I loved the robes and the necklace!), and Toby and

Dad stayed at home. Over the years, Mum made noises about being upset by much of what went on in organized religion, but she seemed to take prayer very seriously. She'd kneel before a service began to have a bit of her own time with her eyes closed, and it always looked like a big mental exertion. She'd press the thumb and forefinger of one hand against her eyeballs and really lean into it, stretching the tendons at the nape of her neck. It never looked like a moment of calm.

I went to college at Indiana University, and attended the Episcopal church in Bloomington, singing in the choir. My journal from those years is full of anguish and confusion about what God allowed to happen, and who was chosen for his understanding. Indiana is in the Bible Belt, remember, and people were pretty vocal at that time, the early 1980s, about homosexuals. I was befriended (a.k.a. targeted) by some people in my Chinese class who saw me as a believer, but not Born Again, and pressured me to go through that canal. I have a terrible memory of sitting at a table with them in the student union, trying to stick up for the way I'd been raised, ending up weeping with them praying around me. Then, one Sunday when I was twenty years old, something told me not to repeat the Nicene Creed with the rest of the congregation. I stood near the altar with the choir and looked out at the people reciting the lines that summarized our faith. I just listened to the rhythmic rumble of the words they spoke, and they all sounded completely insane. It was like being the only sober person at a party, and the faith sitting in my chest was sucked out of me and flew out over their heads and disappeared.

When I finished college, Mum was even more furious about organized religion, and particularly unimpressed by the burden placed on low-income families by the Catholic church's ban on contraception. She no longer attended church, other than on Christmas and sometimes on Easter.

By the end of her life, she had become an atheist, so while she was polite to the pushy woman who stepped into her room a few weeks after her arrival at PRH, she wasn't receptive.

A lay minister
Eucharist in her shoulder bag
Mum sends her packing

(APRIL 21)

Her giving up of any belief in a higher power may have been influenced by how philosophically my father exited his life, but I think it had more to do with Mum's curious mind and her fascination with the natural world. I think she had come to embrace being a temporary repository for the building blocks of the universe. At PRH we discussed the fact that mass could neither be created nor destroyed, as one does, and it led us to Lucretius (c. 99-55 B.C.).

Never a dull mo
Today we talked Lucretius
Ex nihilo, zip
(APRIL 23)

She had me bring a slim red volume of verse from her apartment – Dorothea Wender's *Roman Poetry: From the Republic to the Silver Age.* Reading it out loud to each other was amazing. It fed Mum's mind for a little of each day, with the section of translations of the Epicurean Lucretius' *De Rerum Natura* (*On the Nature of Things*) jibing with what Mum's outlook seemed to be:

No thing turns into nothing, but all things
Turn back at death into their natural seeds.
The rains may perish when the father sky
Pours them into the lap of mother earth,
But shining grain grows up to take their place;
Tree branches bloom and grow and swell with fruit;
And from this grain and fruit the race of men
And beasts is fed, and we see fertile towns
Blossom with children, and the leafy woods
Sing with the sound of baby birds, and cows
Lay down the tiring burden of their bodies
Throughout the fertile pastures; shining milk
Flows from their swollen udders, while the calves,
Their young brains tipsy from the heady drink,
Lustfully leap on shaky legs, and play
Over the tender grass. Therefore, no thing

Which is, can ever perish totally,
Since Nature makes one thing out of another,
And lets no thing be born unless she is
Helped at its birth by the death of something else.

Even so, when my father was dying, he promised Mum that if it was possible to visit her, he would. Very frequently in the months following his death, and intermittently in the years since then, she enjoyed attributing the good things that happened to her to his interference. It used to irk me, this departure from what I thought she believed, and I couldn't always bite my tongue when it happened, to the point that one time when she'd been joyful about Dad's role in a bit of good fortune, I asked her why good fortune couldn't just be good fortune. She looked me in the eye and said, "Alison, I know. I know it's probably nothing to do with Dad. But it's fun for me to feel it." Of course it was. Not my finest moment, that one.

A handsome black-and-white photo of Dad stood facing her in a silver frame on the small chest of drawers opposite the foot of her bed at PRH. A couple of the nurses thought he resembled Paul Newman so strongly that they would greet it with "Good morning, Paul" when they arrived each day. On Monday, June 3rd, four days before she died, while eating some very nice-looking blueberry pancakes, Mum said that one of them had told her that Dad was waiting for her. "But I said," she continued, speaking like a matter-of-fact child and pushing a sticky mouthful onto her fork with her fingers, "he's dead." After a pause she shrugged and added, "But then I thought ... Why not?"

NO LONG FACES

No Long Faces was the rule, from well before the flashing lights, well before the garbled writing, the incomplete thoughts, the shaky hands, the shuffling. That had been the rule, in fact, for life. "Buck up" was a favorite recommendation in hard times.

Mum didn't go straight to "No long faces" when she learned in April 2018 that the cancer hadn't budged from her liver and she'd probably start feeling rotten in about three months. She and Toby and I had a perfectly nice lunch in the hospital café. There was no gnashing of teeth, no tears. The sense was more of surprise. We all went back to Toby's for that night. I told Mum I'd finish her novel for her, knowing that she felt its incompleteness keenly. That would have been a difficult task, as it was so very her. I'm grateful it didn't fall to me, in the end.

The first people she told at Linden Ponds about her prognosis post-immunotherapy were The Nurses. They came into her apartment walking slowly, grim-faced, and were immediately given their instructions on how to interact with her. By the time they reached the couch they'd lightened up, picked up the pace. And that's how it stayed. It was very moving, and instructive, to observe how Mum's friends acceded to her wishes, in ways that worked for them as well.

Mary Ann, for example. She brought her years of sketch journals to show Mum, in the early weeks at PRH. She also often brought chocolate, or crackers from Trader Joe's to replenish Mum's stock, and she settled into a role she might not have expected at the outset – that of florist. She kept Mum in roses, and jonquils, and carnations, continually tending to the bower she created with arrangements on the small chest and others on the table in the bay window. Mum had always enjoyed the sound of someone else pottering around, finding it relaxing. Mary Ann can't have known that. She would come in carrying colorful emblems of their mutual love of gardens and gardening, and there would be some chat. Sometimes Mary Ann would be joined by Mike McPherson, her very genial husband (and the very talented designer of this book). Mary Ann would take the

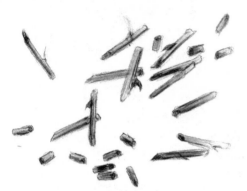

vase of flowers she'd arranged a few days before and refresh the stems in the little sink in Mum's bathroom, giving the vase a wash as well. She'd trim the stems of the new blooms, having scrounged another vase from a volunteer.

She brought Mum some flowering bulbs in April, and as the ninth anniversary of Dad's death approached, Mum requested that Mary Ann and Mike take her to their house so the bulbs could be planted in his memory. I took advantage of Mum having nice things in her schedule to visit Jane in DC that weekend, and Mary Ann sent me an email with photos of the event. Mum was on a plastic lawn chair, wrapped in a big blue comforter with a bright red beret on her head and a bright red scarf around her neck, grinning from ear to ear. Mary Ann, in a bright red hooded jacket, is crouched by the flower bed, arms spread and grinning for the photo as well. She wrote to me that once the flowers were planted, they all stood side by side, facing the ocean. "Then we all shouted, 'JIM! Love to you forever!' at Valerie's prompt."

After a particularly charming visit with Mum in early May, Mary Ann sent me a write-up of the moment. Here's some of it, in which you can see how she and Mike rolled with Mum's moods:

> Valerie asked Mike if he has read translations of Molière by Richard Wilbur. No said Mike but he has read Racine's 'Phaedra' in his translation. By now I had changed the roses' water and was crouched on the floor trimming the stems. I said the one whiter than soap was drooping. V said Wilbur is a poet, too. He wrote her favorite poem of all. What poem? "Love Calls Us to the Things of This World". She said something I didn't catch about "laundry." I asked Mike to find the poem online, and then I asked Valerie to read it. Valerie asked Mike to read it, and he said he would.

Love Calls Us to the Things of This World

The eyes open to a cry of pulleys,
And spirited from sleep, the astounded soul
Hangs for a moment bodiless and simple
As false dawn.
Outside the open window
The morning air is all awash with angels.

Some are in bed-sheets, some are in blouses,
Some are in smocks: but truly there they are.
Now they are rising together in calm swells
Of halcyon feeling, filling whatever they wear
With the deep joy of their impersonal breathing;

Now they are flying in place, conveying
The terrible speed of their omnipresence, moving
And staying like white water; and now of a sudden
They swoon down in so rapt a quiet
That nobody seems to be there.
                              The soul shrinks

From all that it is about to remember,
From the punctual rape of every blessèd day,
And cries,

        "Oh, let there be nothing on earth but laundry,
Nothing but rosy hands in the rising steam
And clear dances done in the sight of heaven."

Yet, as the sun acknowledges
With a warm look the world's hunks and colors,
The soul descends once more in bitter love
To accept the waking body, saying now
In a changed voice as the man yawns and rises,

   "Bring them down from their ruddy gallows;
Let there be clean linen for the backs of thieves;
Let lovers go fresh and sweet to be undone,
And the heaviest nuns walk in a pure floating
Of dark habits,
                keeping their difficult balance."

It was unfamiliar to Mike, and I could follow the words but not whole images. When he finished I asked Valerie if she would read it next, and she said she might not be able to get through it. In spite of messages popping over it onscreen, she read it like a song she had always sung, beautifully, handing the phone to Mike a few times to clear the interference when the touch screen misbehaved in her unaccustomed hands, then going on.

This time I got the picture flowing together from the images and that it is about grace brought on by seeing real laundry on waking. I said the best line for me was "The soul shrinks From all that it is about to remember".

I put as many shortened roses as seemed comfortable in the big vase and asked if I could empty tired flowers from a small vase and put the overage in it. She handed me a tiny parched flowering plant, Kalanchoe, and asked if I thought it needed to be planted outside. I said it was strictly a houseplant, and I took it out to water. She dithered saying she wasn't sure she likes having the dahlia, stopped short of having me remove it. I trimmed off some past blooms and leaves and watered it with a paper cup from the bathroom, part full as if for a sudden need to drink.

A very thin tall woman about our age with long dry platinum hair bounced in, and I tested whether she was a pal of Valerie's I might have met. She declared she is a volunteer on Fridays, and can prepare the mix, holding up V's tonic bottle and two limes, apologizing that only a nurse can dispense the gin.

She asked Valerie how she wanted her drink. "One slice of lime. Ice."

I asked about the weekend. Toby is coming tomorrow, no idea what is Sunday's program. I looked at the clock, 5:30, and V looked at it piteously. I could feel her carpet rolling up with us still standing on it. I stood up, and relieved she said now she could call Jane at the expected time. She and we said we would see each other soon. You call or we will. We gave her kisses and hurried out.

Mum had a bosom buddy in Massachusetts named Sarah with whom she was similar in many ways: British, girls' boarding school, married to an American many years older than she, an equal blend of Monty Python and Mary Poppins, and managing cancer. An actress, this Sarah brought news of performances of *Shear Madness* and the highs and lows of auditions for other shows. She also cuddled Mum, climbing on the bed to do so. She'd stop by on her way to the theater or when doing errands. How strange it was, and what a privilege, to watch those two get physical. I remember Mum saying to me many years before, about a different friend, "She tells me she loves me all the time. It makes me uncomfortable. I don't tell girls I love them. I'm *English*." And yet there she was, hearing it said by her pal on every visit, and saying it back, lifting her arms for hugs and her face for kisses.

The 'Englishness' was learned behavior, of course. I felt so strongly that Mum was returning to her factory settings, letting go of her sharp edges, her harsh judgments, the burden of 'taste'. She'd told me once that cutting my toast into triangles rather than rectangles was low class. Now toast was just a good thing, however it came.

Friends who were too far away or too busy for frequent visits found their ways too. The friend who'd come from England in March figured out how to use FaceTime, and so did Mum. A friend in DC, who had visited Linden Ponds bearing fragrant flowers, continued to send flowers by emailing photos of the lush peonies in his garden and the lush bodies on his favorite gay beach. Another great pal sent emails for me to regale Mum with, turning something as unassuming as a commute to work into a picaresque adventure.

Bruce, who designed *The West Indian*, visited two more times from New Hampshire.

There's more than that to the story of Bruce, and it's worth telling here, because I struggled with it for a while, and then it became a good example of how good, sensitive friends tune in. To tell the story, we have to go back in time a bit, and we have to go to France.

During a trip to Paris over a decade ago, I saw a petite old woman skip out of a Métro train and across the platform to sit on the lap of a tall old man who awaited her there. They'd obviously met in this joyous way before, as the train doors opened directly opposite where he sat. I'd never seen anything like it in my life, and didn't expect that I ever would again. But then Bruce arrived at my brother's for dinner and an overnight stay, late in 2018, and after greeting him at the door my 79-year-old widowed mother skipped into the kitchen with the same childlike spring.

Before dinner, Bruce joined in quizzing my youngest niece on mass, volume and density, and in listening to her play the clarinet. When we all sat down to eat, he said how much he loved being folded into the moment. How lovely for you, I thought, sincerely. Bruce lives and works in a secluded barn, but now he was among three generations of females. That would certainly make a pleasant change, especially if you were sweet on one of them. Yes, I thought, how nice.

But during dinner I considered him across the table. My mother had described him to me as having my husband's coloring. And he did – or the coloring my husband will eventually have. Bruce is about 15 years older than we are, and nearly ten years younger than my mother was. My terminally ill mother. He was also my husband's height, and my father's. Like my husband and my father, he had blue eyes. I considered him and his conversation – the way he chimed in with good stories from childhood, youth, international study and professional striving. I watched him put a hand on my mother's shoulder and take it off again. I waited for him to ask me a question, and he never did. Either that was his way, or he was just letting me consider him rather than actively considering me. Maybe he was nervous. Whatever the case, when we stood up from the table, I found I was only on the very outer edge of whatever folding he had felt. That was my mother's fault. She had taught me to show an interest in people, and to judge them harshly if they didn't do the same.

Mum took Bruce upstairs to show him where he'd be sleeping. She was also staying overnight, in the guest room on the second floor. Bruce and I were to be in facing rooms on the top floor, in my nieces' single beds. The girls were at college. I was mortified. Catherine asked me in a whisper how long the two had been an item. I had no idea. He'd been coming up in conversation for a while, but my mother had a wide range of interesting and loving friends with whom she exchanged visits. I told her that I'd received a short email from him about a month before, telling me he thought my mother was the bee's knees and he hoped we'd meet sometime. I also told her that Mum had recently referred to him as her 'sort-of boyfriend'. That was all I knew.

I went digging. A search for his name in my emails found one where my mother described a visit to his barn, a four-hour journey from her home. They'd eaten delicious risotto and listened to vinyl – the sort of music my father had loved – for hours. "It really took me back to the days when Jim and I did this," she wrote, and I heard only the Jim, not the Bruce. That email was over a year old.

When we all went to bed, I stared up at the hundreds of fluorescent stars on my niece's ceiling, wondering who was feeling what in which room, certain only of my own discomfort in managing my disputing Siamese twins of love and alarm.

There'd been a sort-of boyfriend before, you see. Within in a year of my father's death in 2010, my mother had a torrid fling. No matter how often I expressed my desire not to know about the approaching storm, the storm itself, or the dismay in the wake of his two-timing, she still needed to splash me with it. I realize now that my wording didn't come across as strong to her, no matter how assertive I had felt it was. Pushing back at all felt like a step across a chasm to me. I never clearly said, "That is for you to talk to your friends about," maybe because I'd tried that in high school when she'd done some traumatic oversharing, and it hadn't gone well. It never made sense to her that I didn't want to know.

The warmth between Mum and Bruce was not a wildfire out of control. I could see that, even though it made her skip. It seemed in no way unwise, especially once I figured out that they were cozy with each other months before her diagnosis of terminal melanoma. He was clearly a good man; I believed he would not hurt her. But I also believed he'd want to come to her memorial celebration when she was gone. To be comfortable with that, I'd need to like him. And I didn't want to like him.

An hour after we'd gone to bed, the smoke alarm on the top landing started shrieking. When I opened my door, Toby was climbing the stairs in his boxers. I held a wobbly desk chair for him to climb on and struggle with the wires. Bruce opened his door a crack and said, "Low battery?" with a smile, and I smiled back at him, and he withdrew. He was also in his boxers. Nipples, the eyes of the chest, stand out even in low light. I wondered as I stood next to Toby's hairy thigh, steadying the chair, *Will I be flanked by these two men at my mother's grave?*

Once Bruce had left the following morning, I went for a jog around a reservoir. On the path was a piece of paper that must have blundered over from the nearby middle school. It was titled "Conversations", and listed twelve prompting questions. Looking for a reason not to warm to Bruce, I accordingly felt that any of these questions, except "Do you have a Halloween costume for later?", could have led to conversation that would have helped me want to spend time with him again. Middle school students were being taught to ask conversation-nudging questions. Where were his *manners*?

When I did see Bruce again, though, I was grateful to him beyond measure. He had been midwife to *The West Indian*, and then once I was in Massachusetts, he twice made the four-hour trip to visit my mother in hospice, staying overnight in her apartment. We had a glass of wine together before we retired, and he asked me question after question, about me. This time, though, I wouldn't have cared if he hadn't. My mother had been working on that novel on and off for over three decades. It was her heart's desire to finish and publish, and Bruce made that happen, and my mother went into hospice care with an enormous sense of accomplishment and a peaceful heart. Bruce made her skip. He was friendly in the face of my fierce self-protectiveness. On those two visits to PRH he held my mother in his strong arms. He loved her, and then, with the most beautiful manners, when I told him she was no longer receiving visitors, he stepped aside with grace, sending email messages to her address that simply said "LOVE! LOVE! LOVE!". I knew those messages weren't just for Mum.

Mum instructed us that there were to be no long faces at her memorial either. But that's for the chapter called "Celebration".

First, she has to die.

ABSOLUTELY DELICIOUS

On Friday, May 31st, Toby visited Mum while I waited at her apartment for the arrival of my daughter, Kiri, from New York. I'd told Kiri that if she wanted to visit again while her granny was coherent, it would be best to come soon. Toby sent me an email with the subject line 'Sleepwalk':

[Mum stirs and seems to want to go pee.]

ME: Do you want to go to the bathroom?

MUM: [bright-eyed, smiling] Yes.

ME: Shall I get a nurse to help?

MUM: [hauling herself upright]: No, no. I'm going to the bathroom but I'm not going to the bathroom.

ME: ...?

[She continues to get up.]

ME: Here, let me help. If you need to pee, maybe I should go get a nurse to help? Would you like that?

MUM: No, no. I'm going to the bathroom but I'm not going to the bathroom. Do you see?

ME: ...?

[We get her into the walker, and she starts shuffling purposefully over to the bathroom.]

ME: [opening the bathroom door, turning on the light] Do you need to pee? I'd be happy to help.

MUM: [stops, looks around, takes stock of the situation]: No, no. I'm going to the bathroom but I'm not going to the bathroom.

119

ME: Aha. So you don't need to pee?

MUM: No.

ME: Just going for a bit of a walk?

MUM: That's right.

ME: So . . . back to bed?

MUM: [bright-eyed, smiling, turning around] Yes.

On the morning of Saturday, June 1st, Toby wrote to me, "I noticed that in her sleep she pretty regularly was wiping her lips off with one hand – going all the way round, almost as if she was trying to make sure there was no lipstick anywhere. It wasn't compulsive or frantic, just periodic, and she never seemed to wake up when she was doing it." I wrote back that afternoon, "Interesting that it's happening more! She did that once when I was with her, maybe yesterday morning, don't remember – when she was awake. I asked her what she was doing, and she didn't know."

Sybil gave Kiri and me a ride to PRH. The moment Kiri walked in, Mum said, "Oh! Are you here to sing to me?" Kiri agreed, with a look at me that told me to skedaddle. How I wish I could have listened, but I left them to it. Kiri's visit was Kiri's visit. We also had a video call with my son, Linus, in Los Angeles that day – three generations of women, squashed together on Mum's bed, talking to her one grandson. Marvelous.

On Sunday, June 2nd, Toby brought Catherine and all three daughters to PRH, and the youngest, Sage, nearly twelve, and I assembled our clarinets and practiced one more time before playing Mum a little duet by Schumann. (When I'd arrived in the morning I'd said, "I'm going to wear your clothes today, because I couldn't fit mine in my backpack with my clarinet." To which she'd replied, "Then what am I going to wear?")

That afternoon, after they all left, Mum's anxiety began. She dreamed that blood was coming out of her ears, and it frightened her so much she cried. I told her that wasn't going to happen; she was just going to sleep and sleep and sleep. I remembered Mum telling me that when I was fractious as a little child, all she had to do was take me outdoors and I'd be cheerful again. That had been very helpful advice with my own children, and now I leaned on it once more. I asked the nurses to put Mum in the wheelchair – I was no longer able to manage the transfers myself – and Mum and I went outside in the sunshine for a while, looking at the beautiful irises in the side garden. Once back inside, I brushed her teeth and the nurses washed her and put her in a clean nightgown, and she went back to sleep.

That was the day Mum started taking Ativan in the daytime. She'd been taking half a tablet at night since a hospice nurse's visit to her apartment soon after I'd arrived in March. Mum didn't like taking drugs any more than she liked visiting doctors and hospitals. She had been able to avoid statins for a while by taking red yeast rice capsules, and had avoided blood-pressure medication completely by eating less salt and using an electronic device once a day to help calm her by regulating her breathing. But she had a positive (well, positive enough) association with Ativan to sign on for that. Not only had she seen how it had helped my father, she had also taken his surplus tablets to help herself through the anxious times after his death. He had been her Ativan, and once he was gone, she needed the real thing.

The goal was to keep anxiety at bay. And not just Mum's. People were still saying she might have a few more weeks to go, but Toby was growing uncomfortable with being nearly an hour away, so he decided to stay at Linden Ponds with me from Tuesday, June 4th, no matter how long the end was going to take.

I had an early call from Pam, one of the great nurses who had come to know Mum so well, on the morning of Monday the 3rd, though, saying that Mum had woken up anxious, and had asked for me to come. I biked over as fast as I could. When I came through the door of Mum's room she reacted with renewed tears, reaching up to me with her skinny arms like a little child. I put down my helmet and backpack, took off my shoes, and climbed on the bed to hold her. Again, she spoke in the voice of a child. "Pam says I've been such a trooper, but I don't feel like a trooper." She showed me an obviously malignant mole on her forearm that, strangely, neither of us had noticed before. She didn't use words as she pointed to it, more of a mewl of distress. I covered it with my palm and told her it couldn't hurt her now.

Pam had given her Ativan when she woke up upset, and when she began to calm down, I went to the kitchen to give the volunteer there her order. I hadn't been able to reach Toby on the phone, but he sent me an email when he was able to look at his phone. He was on an exam table having some earwax removed (if you are in your fifties perhaps this sort of thing won't surprise you) and wondered if he should get up and dash to Hingham. I told him not to cut his appointment short, but to come as quickly as he could. He said he'd go home and throw a bag together first, so he could stay.

It was during this breakfast that Mum shrugged and said, "Why not?" about the idea that Dad might be waiting for her in the ether. When she was nearly finished, Pam came in to see her, standing at the end of the bed. Mum said to me, "Shall we work on the announcement?" I looked at Pam, who didn't appear to realize what Mum meant. I turned back to Mum and asked, "The announcement of your death, you mean?"

"Yes."

"Oh my God," Pam said to Mum. "You are amazing."

I told Mum that Toby was on his way and would probably like to be involved. She thought about that for a moment, then said, "Okay, I'll have a little more, then," organizing another mouthful of pancake.

We didn't end up writing the announcement that day, because her thinking rapidly became less clear, as did her words. But we'd had conversations about it in the previous weeks, some of which I had recorded on my phone. I'm so glad I did this. I love listening to those recordings, much more than I like looking at photographs. The voice is made by breath, and breath is life.

Once Toby was there and we were settled in for the day, she said, "I can't remember what I was crying about." The mood lightened. She told us we'd need to bring a knife along when we transported her ashes to Maine to mingle with Dad's, as the plastic bag Dad's were in was very thick and would be hard to open. She slept a lot, but had a bit more talking to do. At one point in the late afternoon she asked us, "Do you think I need the, um...the, um...Do you think I need the, um...the stew pot?"

After the moment it took to decide that what she'd said couldn't be interpreted in any other way than itself, I said, "I don't think so, Mum." Toby said, "Pretty sure you don't need the stew pot."

She nodded. Toby and I didn't know what to say after that. Mum must have replayed the conversation in a coherent part of her mind, as she broke the tension by making fun of herself. "Stew pot," she said. "Heh heh heh heh."

Later in the day she was sitting up in bed with us sitting on the bed on either side of her. Her eyes were wide open, like a preverbal toddler.

She brought her hand to her chin and then to her cheek, squeezing and pulling her fingers away, saying "Nnnyip" as she did so. I wondered if she thought there was something there, something difficult to remove – cancer? We told her there was nothing on her face.

I was wearing a white top with navy stripes. She became intrigued by it, and gently reached out a hand, grasping for it near the neckline, but she needed a few tries before actually taking the fabric between her fingers. It was as if she was seeing the stripes in 3D. To this, there was also nothing to say. She was fascinated, and smiling, so we watched, and wondered. It was very, very weird. It was also very cute. I once had an encounter with a baby orangutan. It was a bit like that.

Now there's Ativan
Enormous, face-cracking yawns
Head turning slowly
(JUNE 3)

She wished the Ativan would do more than calm her down. She wanted it to knock her out. Still, she didn't get cranky. As evening drew on, she wanted to remain conversant, but she was finding words difficult to understand, and began saying a sweet, very British "Right" in answer to just about everything we said to her. Jeannie, the night nurse, came on at 7. She had talked with the day nurses about how Mum was, of course, but told us all that she'd ask Mum some yes-or-no questions to hear from Mum herself as well. She had to get used to "Right" rather than "Yes", first. Mum hadn't had any lunch, hadn't shown interest in food at all since breakfast. Jeannie asked if she wanted some dinner, some ice cream, any snacks. Mum was non-committal. Then Jeannie had a brilliant idea and asked her if she'd like a gin and tonic. I can't remember if Mum actually said yes in answer; all I remember is that she sparkled. The yes was clear to us all.

Toby raised the head of her bed and positioned her overbed table. The G&T arrived with its slice of lime, and I got the bag of rice crackers from the snack drawer. I helped her drink, and fed her crackers. She didn't talk, just drank a glug of cocktail and then opened her mouth for more crackers, like a baby in her highchair. Taking the glass from her mouth after a few minutes of this I asked, "Is that nice?"

"Absolutely delicious."

After a few more minutes, a mountain of crackers and about half her drink, we realized she was chewing with her eyes closed. We told her we were going to lay her back down again. She slept.

So that was her last meal. And those were her last words.

But there were still a few days to go.

THIS PART STINKS

On Tuesday, June 4th, I wrote to Mary Ann: "Mum seems to have passed through 'terminal agitation' last night, and is now peaceful, as in, zonked even when eyes open. All the signs are there for departure in a few days, if not less."

I was wrong. What we'd seen in the last few days had been anxiety. Agitation was about to begin in earnest.

Catherine drove down for a final moment alone with Mum, who often didn't seem to be fully asleep because she kept bringing a shaking hand to her throat. She gave no response when we asked if she was uncomfortable, or was thirsty, just kept repeating the gesture. I repositioned her delicate necklace, a gift from my father that she never took off, but the movement continued. We could no longer understand her, and we couldn't tell if she knew we were there. We had to try to accept that we couldn't comfort her.

By the end of the day, however, she was sleeping deeply. I wrote to my godmother, "Toby and I feel relatively confident going back to Linden Ponds to sleep rather than here with her, as her breathing is still regular."

I didn't know what I was talking about, but you hold on to things and offer them to others. We just needed a break.

We returned early on the 5th, Wednesday. Mum had her eyes closed when we arrived, but was turning her head from side to side as if straining to hear. When we greeted her and kissed her, she emitted the sweetest, tenderest set of "Aaaah"s, and set to snoring. It was so good to know that she was aware of us. She slept peacefully all day. I took over her Kindle and began reading Susan Orlean's *The Library Book*, finding strange highlights in the text – "only seven stories high, which was the case with the Goodhue building", "case like the library fire. The wobbliness", a reminder that, while Mum had been able to read and enjoy it, her undependable fingers had tripped things up from time to time. Phrases got highlighted when she was trying to tap the page forward.

Mum cooed again on our arrival the next day, and she seemed to settle right down, but it was clear she was having more trouble breathing, snoring into a half-cough, half-moan, again raising a trembling hand to her neck, and sometimes to her cheek. Pam told us that when she had arrived that morning, Mum had been gesturing in a way that made Pam uncomfortable – a surfeit of agitation – so she gave Mum some of the anti-psychotic Haldol. Pam introduced morphine into the mix on that day as well. Toby and I were fully supportive of that, and knew that Mum was too, having regretted not doing more to make Dad comfortable when he was dying.

Despite all these drugs, though, Mum remained unsettled. Other than reacting to our arrival, she didn't try to communicate with any of us, except for a moment when Pam had been in to check on her and we discussed giving her more morphine. Pam was going to have to make a call to see if she could up the dose, but she warned us, "This part stinks. It's terrible that they have to go through it, but they do." When she left to make the call, Mum turned her head, eyes still closed, toward the door, and vocalized something, seeming to call out to Pam. To me, it looked like, "Get me that drug. Please, oh please, knock me out."

I had imagined that hospice care would mean that Mum could be knocked out. I didn't remember this same sort of tossing and turning in my father, the same desire for more drugs. But I realized that I hadn't factored in Dad's fast. By the time he was a few days from dying, he hadn't eaten in eleven days. He was totally depleted.

There are limits to the opioids they can give. They're not allowed to kill you, of course, even if that's what you want. Pam told us about the news from the day before, about an Ohio doctor charged with 25 counts of murder in opioid deaths (fentanyl, in his case), underlining that her hands were tied. And chafing.

Mary Ann emailed me a vibrant portrait of Mum done in cardinal red, with grass-green eyes. The background was grass green, canary yellow, and royal blue. It was so full of energy, Mum seemed to move. I sent an update in reply: "Heart rate still strong. Heart too strong, in fact."

Toby and I caught up on email and editing work, played backgammon, stroked Mum, and told her nice things.

Later in the afternoon, deeply unsettled by Mum's struggle, I had a phone conversation with a friend who is a palliative care doctor, which helped me understand that the palliative medicines couldn't just settle Mum into easy breathing. As Pam had said, the struggle was requisite in a case like Mum's. She was in the death canal, as she had once been in the birth canal. In a follow-up text I wrote, "She's not necessarily suffering, right? Looks like suffering, but perhaps not on a conscious level for her." She replied, "Not necessarily suffering. Just the machinery having a hard time as it's slowing down. Not her self. Just her body."

Just her body. Not her self. That was incredibly helpful.

Toby and I took turns going for runs in the woods.

Then we needed to decide whether to stay or to go, a decision especially difficult for Toby, as the next day was Sage's birthday. Pam ventured a guess to help us – she didn't think Mum would die within the next eight to twelve hours, but could go within the next twenty-four. Toby took a chance. He dropped me at Linden Ponds, and I picked up the key to Audrey and Mike's car.

Toby called me at 5:35 the next morning. PRH had contacted him to say that Mum had shifted to another state and it was best that we be there. I dressed and brushed my teeth. I think I threw some food in a bag. I drove over.

The mornings had been dark and cold when I'd arrived in March and the deciduous trees hadn't budded yet, but the sun rose at 5:08 on June 7th, and I drove in light, flanked by greenery. In addition to the regular wildlife around PRH, the seasonal, ruby-throated hummingbirds had arrived, and jetted between the feeders near the side porch and the foliage under Mum's window.

I was there by about 6:00, Toby roughly 6:30. He'd seen Sage briefly the night before, but she'd have her birthday without him.

Mum was indeed different. Her breathing was no longer such a raspy struggle, no longer the upsetting air hunger of the previous days. It was more of a snore and a sigh, largely regular. It appeared purely mechanical. She lay unmoving on her back, her head dropped to the side and down, as if she was nodding off in a chair. The bottoms of her feet were purple. Hypoxemia. I remembered her showing me the blooms of purple on Dad's lily-white feet (he'd never been much of a sandal man – at least, not without socks). Now I wanted to tell him about Mum's.

Maybe I ate while I was waiting for Toby. I don't remember. I know that the light in the room grew and grew. When he arrived, he pulled up a chair next to me by the bed. Mum hadn't responded to either arrival. Toby scrolled through things on his phone. I wanted to sing to Mum. I'd sung to Dad, once, in his last days. I'd been taking singing lessons then, and had a song in mind for him: "Orpheus with his Lute", with words from Shakespeare's *Henry III*, set to music by Ralph Vaughan Williams.

> *Orpheus with his lute made trees,*
> *And the mountain tops that freeze,*
> *Bow themselves when he did sing:*
> *To his music plants and flowers*
> *Ever sprung; as sun and showers*
> *There had made a lasting spring.*
> *Every thing that heard him play,*
> *Even the billows of the sea,*
> *Hung their heads, and then lay by.*
> *In sweet music is such art,*
> *Killing care and grief of heart*
> *Fall asleep, or hearing, die.*

He had been fretting, wanting to get out of bed, and the song settled him into a snooze.

I'd only had the clarinet duet in mind for Mum, and that was done. It was a bit late for singing, really, but I wanted to, and went with the first song that came to mind, "It's Never Too Late to Fall in Love", by Sandy Wilson, from his 1954 musical, *The Boy Friend*. Mum had been in an amateur production of it, with Dad on piano in the orchestra, when we were living in St. Croix in the late Sixties, and I listened to the record all through my childhood. The song is a duet between a young woman and a much older man, so I did both voices. Toby smirked.

I may be too old to run a mile
Run a mile?
Yes, run a mile
But there's one thing I still do very well
I may be too old to climb a stile
Climb a stile?
Yes, climb a stile
But there's one thing at which I still excel
Although my hair is turning grey
Yes, it's rather grey!
I still believe it when I say
Well, what do you say?
It's never too late to have a fling
For autumn is just as nice as spring
And it's never too late to fall in love
Boop-a-doop, boop-a-doop, boop-a-doop
It's never too late to wink an eye
I'll do it until the day I die
And it's never too late to fall in love
Boop-a-doop, boop-a-doop, boop-a-doop
If they say I'm too old for you
Then I shall answer "Why, sir,
One never drinks the wine that's new
The old wine tastes much nicer"
A gentleman never feels too weak
To pat a pink arm or pinch a cheek
And it's never too late to fall in love
Sez who? *Sez me*
Sez you? *Sez we.*
Sez both of us together
...etc.

Very silly. But it was hard not to feel slap-happy, punch-drunk, giddy with uncertainty and the need to fill the space with sounds other than the heavy burr and sough of Mum's breath. It felt like she could go on like that for a long time. Toby wondered if he might have been able to have a birthday breakfast with Sage.

A trio of male wild turkeys on the lawn strutted and gobbled for a trio of females in the field beyond the fence.

Toby suggested backgammon, so we moved the chairs closer to the window and on either side of the overbed table, where the game was. I put on a mixed CD of our dad playing jazz, and we set up the game. Dooby-dooby-dooby, gobble-gobble, click-click, burr. Dooby-dooby, gobble, burr, click, click, click. We got used to the sounds, concentrated on the game. When we were about halfway through it, Toby looked up at the sound of…nothing, coming from Mum. I met his eyes. We flew out of our chairs, dragging them to either side of the bed. Toby turned off the CD. He put his hand on Mum's chest, and I took her left hand in my left, wrapping my right fingers around her wrist. I could feel the fluttering pulse. She breathed again. We didn't. Silence. She breathed. Silence. "Her heart's not beating," Toby whispered. "Her pulse is still fluttering," I replied, and then felt the tiny butterflies under my fingers fly away. I told Toby her pulse was gone, and watched the rims of his eyelids go pink around blue eyes open as wide as they would go.

CELEBRATION

Our eyes welled, and we looked at our quiet mother, feeling the depths of the silence. Gobble-gobble-gobble-gobble! went the turkeys in a lusty chorus, and we sputtered into wet giggles at the sublime ridiculousness. We laughed and hugged, cried and exhaled, then sat back down in our chairs and put our hands back on our mother. We stroked her arms and face, talking about how much she would have loved that moment, how Monty Python couldn't have scripted it better.

It was about ten past eight.

Eventually, we pressed the button on the side of the bed, and a tender trio of nurses came in and hugged us. They would have seen the end of Mum's life on their video monitor, but they wouldn't have heard the turkeys the way we did, so we told them about that, and we continued to tell that story for the next days as we informed people Mum had achieved lift-off. It made them laugh, and we laughed along. I am so grateful to those birds.

The head nurse pronounced Mum dead, and the three of them left us to take as long as we needed to with her. We sat back down and put our hands on our mother again. It felt wrong not to be touching her. She still looked like Mum, and felt like Mum. Toby had asked me earlier if I wanted time on my own with her, and now I found I did, so he went downstairs. That moment was a huge benefit to me, because I realized that I didn't want to be consoled. That's not something people talk about much – the burden, however light, of another person's caring. Alone with my mother's body, I could throw my arms across her and press my forehead against her chest and wail, lift my head and talk, and lay it against her again, and no one would be wondering what to do or when to do it.

When my tears shifted from sobbing to her to sobbing for myself, I texted "Come back?" to Toby.

When we asked the nurses to come back, they returned to wash Mum, and put her in the pale-pink silk robe she'd be cremated in. I had imagined I'd participate in the washing, having found it helpful in my father's case, but I couldn't do it. Toby and I went elsewhere, and sent messages to Mum's friends. When I contacted Audrey, I asked her if she'd be willing to co-host a get-together with us at their apartment, to send Mum off. Mum had told us categorically not to have a memorial service at Linden Ponds. "Those poor people have a memorial service to go to every week," she'd said. She had chosen which photograph of her to put up on the common-room mantelpiece (what she referred to as 'The Wall of Death') when she died, but that was all she wanted. So, we wouldn't have a memorial service, we'd have drinks. I knew that her friends would want to gather, and I knew it would be good for Toby and me to be able to see as many of them as we could in one place rather than having to repeat ourselves in the halls. I also knew that close friends like Audrey would be very glad for something to do.

Once Mum's body had been washed, we began packing up her things, pottering around her as we were accustomed to doing. Spending this much time with her body was important. It felt familiar and easy for a long while, and then, suddenly, I started being surprised by its presence. I was packing up the bathroom, and when I came out it was a shock to see her – it – in the bed. Soon after that, at the same moment, Toby and I felt that she was becoming less recognizable, not grey in the way corpses are so often described, but tinged with yellow, and deeply inert. This is when we knew we'd had enough time with her.

Mum had been keen for us to engage the undertakers who had taken care of Dad's body, so Toby and I had met with them and made our arrangements, telling PRH which company we'd chosen. This meant that when we were ready to set the cremation ball rolling, we merely had to tell the nurses and they made contact with the funeral parlor. While we waited for them, we stood outside the second-floor nurses' station with the available staff, to raise a glass to Mum. We all had tonic and lime, but of course only Toby and I added a splash of gin. We told our favorite Valerie stories – after nine weeks together with her, the nurses and aides had plenty of stories too.

The undertaker arrived, once again a pretty woman, and all of us who'd been having a drink went back to Mum's room to see her a final time. I don't remember what I did or said once I was there. I only remember one of the nurses reaching out her hand to stroke Mum's cheek with a finger. She turned to me with tears in her eyes, and a hug. "I loved her," she said. "I can't do this part," I told her. "I get that," she said, and I ran outside to lie on the grass, unceremoniously leaving Toby to sign what needed signing and watch her body be taken away.

We finished packing up her room, and loaded the cars, and thanked everyone at PRH who was available to thank again. It was mid-afternoon. We went to lunch. As we waited for our seafood sandwiches, hungry and tingling with adrenalin and the beginnings of profound fatigue, Toby said, "Well, we did it."

Yes, indeed. We saw her out, hand in hand with the people of PRH and her friends, all of us guardians along her chosen path.

The next afternoon, we joined Mum's Linden Ponds friends at Audrey and Mike's for cocktails. The night before, Audrey had dreamed that the living room was full of spirits, including Mum's. That afternoon it was certainly full of Mum's spirit, living on in her lively and interesting friends. The gin, which Mum had taught several of the people assembled to appreciate, was flowing. After a period of general conversation, we arranged ourselves in a sort of circle in the living room, with some people sitting and some standing. Toby and I thanked everyone and I read a poem we had found when we went through Mum's memorabilia with her in April. It had been written by her friend the playwright and director Ruth Moore, for her 30th birthday, in July 1969.

Thirty Light Years

This one!
She is so something, this one.
She is "Hah!"
And she is "How now?"
She is a charge of light.
Draw her in straight lines.
Sing her in high notes.

Dance her without bones.
Whatever her years, they will be light years,
Whatever her days, they will be "Hah!" days,
And moonlit "How nows?" sparkling over all.

Mike, bless him, asked the group if anyone had a funny story to tell. Bless him, because it's awkward to be in a circle of open faces with nothing left to say to them.

Nancy stood up, holding her gin, and talked about how irritating it was to watch *Jeopardy* with Mum because she always knew so many of the answers. A Jamaican-American friend who had read *The West Indian* for Mum to test it against his ear, told us how she had brought him a bottle of rum as a thank-you, and had shared a glass with him, taking hers neat. Then a French friend, Maurice, stepped forward. He said he didn't have something funny to relate, but wanted instead to express what an impression both my parents' approaches to death had made on him. Taking real ownership of the end of one's life wasn't at all the norm in France, he told us. When my father chose to stop eating, Maurice asked his doctor if he'd support him doing the same in the face of a debilitating terminal illness. He was very surprised when the doctor said yes. Then he went to the Linden Ponds chaplain with the same question, and the answer was the same. Maurice told us that his view of what was permitted at the end of one's life was changed forever, giving him a greater sense of agency. It really felt to me, watching him make that speech, that he was giving thanks for the knowledge that he'd be able to walk tall, internally if not externally, all the way to the end, with no need to submit to anyone's concept of how it should go, emboldened instead by his own vision of how it *could* go.

Mum had told us in April of 2018 what she wanted to happen after she died. We had traveled down to DC together after her prognosis of three to six months left, and over dinner with good friends she said that we should go to her favorite beach, Nantasket, and do cartwheels and whoop and holler and write her name in the sand, and then have a delicious meal at Jake's, our favorite seafood restaurant nearby. Then she said, "Wait …November…Jake's won't be open. Well, you'll find somewhere else."

It was so good to know what she imagined us doing. My father hadn't expressed any particular vision to us, and as a result we fell in with what Mum wanted – again, something small, including poetry, and also music. Three days after he died, we assembled with poems we'd chosen and written and a portable CD player at the hexagonal deck overlooking one of the quarry ponds that Linden Ponds is named after. The best part of that gathering for me was when Debussy's "Syrinx" was played. It's a four-minute piece for solo flute, named after the song organ of birds. ("Syrinx" can also refer to pan pipes, but listen to a recording of the Debussy piece, and decide which one you think the flute is imitating.) The acoustics of the quarry were excellent, and the sound of the flute rose above us, into the trees, and the birds in the trees set to twittering in response. Then we went out for a Chinese dinner in a lively restaurant with red lamps and a waiter who made us laugh.

Like Dad's friends, and then later Mum's friends, who visited and wrote and called, arranged flowers, baked brownies, and painted portraits while my parents were dying, in our celebrations we were doing us, in a way that expressed our connection to our loved ones, and to each other.

One of the books that Mum had me bring to PRH to read together was *A Manual of Death Education and Simple Burial*, written by Ernest Morgan and published by The Celo Press in 1980. It had been sent to the Harvard Educational Review where she was working as a secretary, and she had kept it since then in an old, monogrammed stationery case along with other interesting keepsakes that didn't have an obvious file in a cabinet.

I read to her now
A slim manual on death
She sits ramrod straight

(MAY 28)

Ernest Morgan was an advocate of simple, dignified, and economical funeral arrangements, and we found his writing both reasonable and touching. One segment early in the book, on accepting the reality of death, rang out:

A civilized way to accept the reality of death is first to discuss it frankly in advance, and to plan intelligently to meet it and, second, to conduct a sensitive and meaningful funeral or memorial service designed to meet the particular needs of the particular family. Then when death does arrive it will not be as a mysterious intruder, but as a guest, usually expected and sometimes even welcomed.

Death is a more positive experience when there are active roles for the survivors. In pioneer times when family and friends built the burial box, placed the body in it, and dug the grave, there was no lack of wholesome participation. Today the professional has been called upon to perform these functions. The one remaining vestige of active participation is the pall bearer. For the most part, family and friends are relegated to the status of spectator. If death in the modern world is to have positive meaning, we need a greater degree of awareness and understanding of it than in the past.

As the weeks in hospice passed and the weather got better and better, and Jake's opened for the season, I felt sustained by the idea that we would be able to do exactly what she hoped we would, and also what we needed to do for ourselves.

The eventual physical and emotional structure of the beach celebration came out of a conversation Toby and I had about what people would be able to get out of an amorphous request to make noise and do gymnastics. Not a whole lot, we thought – especially as few of us remained limber! I thought about who was coming, and set about delegating responsibilities, not only so that we would have a plan, but also because people want something to do – it's a handhold in the storm.

First, I talked to Mary Ann. It was such a boon to have a pair of artist-designers in the group. I proposed that she and Mike take what Mum wanted and see how something could be built with it, so that the group efforts would be less individual, more concerted.

I also talked to the actress in our midst, Sarah, who has a terrific singing voice. Rather than sing separately, we decided to rehearse "Bosom Buddies" from *Mame*, for a bit of comic relief. I'd been collecting poems for people to read as well, and asked Toby and Catherine to read one each.

I struggle with the word 'memorial'. It feels so heavy to me, and heavy with responsibility. "Don't forget," it says, as if you ever could. 'Celebration' pops in the mouth like champagne.

Our beach celebration was set for Monday, June 17th, giving everyone time to arrange their work and travel schedules. Andy flew in from England, Linus flew in from Los Angeles, and Kiri trained up from New York. Toby's middle daughter, Kate, was home from her summer job as a camp counselor, as the 16th was her birthday. Bless her heart, she was willing, after her birthday dinner and cake, for all of us to spend the evening decorating prayer flags provided by Mary Ann with the things we thought of when we thought of Valerie Lester. Mary Ann did the same at her house. It was something to do with our hands. Something to do with our thoughts. Somewhere to put them. Wonderful.

And then, on the 17th, we ate great food, and drank prosecco, all paid for by my aunt Jane, who could only be there in spirit. After lunch we trooped along the beach, stopping to read poems as we sought a space that felt right for noise and construction. Sarah and I belted out "Bosom Buddies", and then Mary Ann and Mike gave us our jobs. Sage, the gymnast among us, was asked to collect stones to establish a cartwheel run, and the rest of the cousins helped her. Mary Ann asked Sarah to lay out a line of small white boxes between the stones, on which she had written our names as well as the pet names Mum had for us. Others of us planted stakes in the sand on which to string up the prayer flags behind the run, and Mary Ann and Mike also unfurled a beautiful long piece of pale blue silk that undulated in the air. Mum almost never left Nantasket Beach, or any beach, without picking up trash, so we also looked around for trash with which to continue that practice – but there wasn't any. While the prayer flags fluttered, Mary Ann handed out the hydrangea canes she had scavenged and we drew the names in the sand that we had used to call Mum – Mum, Mummy, Granny, Annie, Valerie, Val, My Palerie – with Mike writing a beautiful bold VALERIE in the font called Bodoni. We threw our bodies along the cartwheel run. I used to be able to do an effortless cartwheel. I thought it was like riding a bike. Turns out it hurts if you haven't been practicing. Even so, I got back in line and did a round-off, crashing to the ground. We all did what we could, or wanted to do – somersaulting, skipping, vamping, trucking – until it felt like we were done, then we lined up along the run and held hands to shout, "Valerie! Love to you for EVER!" at the ocean and the sky.

That was when the tears came. You can't shout like that without the floodgates bursting.

"Let's go and put our feet in the ocean," I said, once the fantastic group hugs were complete.

Mary Ann took off her clothes.

"You wore a swimsuit??" I said.

"I thought you would!" she replied.

I hadn't even thought of it, which is crazy. I suppose I didn't because she and I had already been swimming at Nantasket, the day after Mum died. I'd known I'd need to be in the water then and had asked Mary Ann to take me. We took turns on her boogie board, and I now love noticing the pale scar on my knee from my first attempt, when I got the technique of standing back up totally wrong and scraped myself on some rocks. It's shaped like lipstick left after a kiss.

I took off my shorts and plunged in with Mary Ann in my t-shirt and panties. The rest of the gang stood ankle deep and chatted.

Do you know the e.e. cummings poem called "maggie and milly and molly and may"? It ends with "For whatever we lose (like a you or a me)/ it's always ourselves we find in the sea". It's true for me, but I'll always find Mum there too.

Once out and starting to dry off, we took smiling group photos, as you would at a wedding or birthday party.

Before we took the construction down, we read one more poem, this time as a group. It was again "Thirty Light Years", by Ruth Moore. I had printed 12 copies, and we stood in a circle and each read out a line. We repeated the first line, loud, in unison, at the end.

Thirty Light Years

This one!
She is so something, this one.
She is "Hah!"
And she is "How now?"
She is a charge of light.
Draw her in straight lines.
Sing her in high notes.
Dance her without bones.
Whatever her years, they will be light years,
Whatever her days, they will be "Hah!" days,
And moonlit "How nows?" sparkling over all.
THIS ONE!

BURYING THE REMAINS

Mum had a possession that Toby and I weren't sure what to do with. It was an ivory statuette, the top half of which was a pair of camels; the bottom half featured an elephant reaching for the leaves of a tree. It was a family heirloom that neither of us fancied inheriting, and we didn't imagine many people were open to ivory these days. I wrote to a friend who is legal specialist for USAID wildlife activity in Asia: "I can't see myself putting it in the rubbish, out of respect for the poor elephant. I'm inclined to give it a proper burial, unless you have another idea from the conservation perspective?" She wrote back that a proper burial sounded like a lovely idea, and recommended including a little ritual to honor the elephant. Then she added, "Also not all ivory is a result of poaching. Some is from elephants that have died a natural death."

I didn't know what constituted a 'proper burial', of course, but I knew I could at least achieve a burial. Toby said it was okay for me to dig a hole in one of the flower beds in his front yard, so I did that, and lay the statuette in it, and said something I was rather pleased with at the time – an apology of sorts, I believe, holding the whole elephant in my mind – but I can't remember a word of now. I covered the figurine with earth, and then I weeded both front beds, because weeding is extremely therapeutic.

We had long known what a proper burial meant to Mum, as she and Dad had bought a plot on Islesboro, Maine well before Dad died, giving themselves a good long time for discussing what sort of stone they'd like to place there. I think there was talk for a while about having two stones, hers with her name and dates and the word 'WORDS' on it, his with name and dates and 'MUSIC'. But the final decision was made for one stone. Dad's name and dates were above Mum's, as he went first. For nine years, it had '1939 –' under Mum's name. We called upon the craftsman who cut their stone, fine lettercutter Douglas Coffin, to complete the carving with '2019'.

Now we must take Mum's ashes there.

We know how to dig Dad up because Mum sent us photos of the stages of burying him:

1. Mum seen from behind in jeans and teal fleece jacket, carrying a red-and-white L.L. Bean tote bag. In it is the blue-and-white Chinese ginger jar she put Dad's ashes in ($5 at a local auction), rather than an urn from the funeral home.

2. Mum with a man, looking at where he is pointing on some papers, no doubt establishing the parameters of the plot.

3. Mum and the man, each with a spade, digging a rectangle by a large cotoneaster bush and a small American flag marking the grave of a veteran. To their right are panels of wood laid on the grass. The ginger jar looks on from behind them.

4. Seen from the other side, Mum is shoveling earth onto the wood, where they have also set aside the turf.

5. Mum has put the ginger jar on a large flat boulder crispy with lichen. She has taken off her fleece to reveal a blue-and-white striped top. She is leaning on the boulder from behind it, with her arms around the jar and her cheek against its shoulder, giving her sweetheart a final hug. The Chinese character on the jar, 囍, has no pronunciation of its own, but is referred to as **shuāng xǐ**, 双喜, meaning double happiness, because it is a doubling of the character for happy. It is used to celebrate weddings, which is, in effect, what Mum is doing in this photograph.

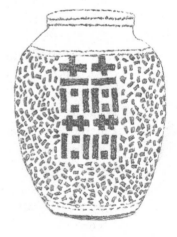

6. The urn is now in the rectangular hole. Mum is kneeling by the hole, leaning over to press both hands against the top of the urn, sending love down through her arms.

7. Mum and the man have refilled the hole and are fitting the turf back on top, tucking Dad in.

Later, once the stone was complete, she sent us a photo of that as well, stark against the trampled grass. And then each summer, she would go back to Islesboro to "give Dad a trim," and she'd write and tell us how things were at the grave, including the development of the pretty Japanese maple tree Jane bought as a tribute. Butterflies of different types often played a role in the experience.

A couple of years before she died, Mum sent us a photo taken straight down, showing us the bottom half of the stone and her feet in orange sandals on some lively grass, as well as a photo of the maple. Her email said, "See that yellow flower? It's directly above the urn! Remember the expression, pushing up daisies? Jim has something else in mind. And no, it's not a dandelion. I'm going to have to look it up. And here's the Japanese maple, Jano. Isn't it looking great? I'm going to ask if it's safe to remove the fence and the bandage now. Stay tuned." She was showing us where to dig when the time came to mingle her ashes with Dad's, not in the jar, but in the earth. And she was having fun with it. Fun! "Stay tuned," she wrote, as if we were on the edge of our seats about whether the fence could be removed.

I didn't think about these emails very much when they came in. Reports from Mum were always lively, whatever the subject. They strike me now as a very active form of loving, and something to be carried forward. She was loving Dad, of course, but she was also loving Toby and me by giving us a familiarity with the place we'd be making our own pilgrimage to (neither of us had visited Islesboro since the memorial jazz concert for Dad in the church by the cemetery). She was loving Jane by showing so much appreciation for the tree. Mum was also loving herself by respecting her feelings of loss and allowing herself as much time as she needed for her visits. While her emails were jolly, I know she suffered. She told me once in a phone call from Islesboro that she had been standing in the kitchen of the house she was staying in, looking out the window, and had suddenly shouted, "Come back! Come back!" I have no doubt that despite the travels and dalliances and achievements of her widowhood, she missed my father every single day. I have no doubt that knowing that death represented an end to her bereavement helped her to welcome it.

In her final missive to us from Islesboro, on August 31, 2018, she wrote:

> I have been meaning to tell you about my lovely visit with Dad. I borrowed gardening tools from Sandy but didn't have to do much trimming round the stone as the new mowing man is doing an excellent job. I did trim around the tree as it still has its anti-deer fence. Then I lay down on the warm tombstone and closed my eyes. When I opened them again, two monarch butterflies were soaring overhead. As I left, I walked past a large white hydrangea bush, and one of the monarchs flew from it and circled my head several times. Once again, a lovely Jim surprise.

Jane didn't like talking about what would happen after she died, fixating instead on how much she still wanted to do before then. Over the years of hospital and assisted-living visits, Mum tried, Toby tried, I tried to get an idea from her of what would please her to imagine, but she was slippery on the subject. Mum eventually got her to state that she'd prefer cremation to a coffin, so we could plan on that, at least. But then what? She once alluded to something she'd fancy, but then scurried back to saying she didn't know, and anyway, she'd be dead, what did it matter? Not only did acknowledging her mortality alarm her, the idea of anyone celebrating her life made her feel shy, and talking about it seemed like self-aggrandizement to her. This was still the case when I visited her in June after Mum died, before I returned to England. So, I wrote her a letter, reminding her what she had said, adding, "Unless we hear from you otherwise, that's what we'll do. But you must feel free to change your mind on this. Your wish is absolutely our command. We will not feel put out by fulfilling your wishes, Jane. We will feel glad, and satisfied." I also asked her if there were poems she'd like read or songs sung.

True to form, Jane couldn't bring herself to respond to this letter, and/or forgot she had received and read it. Sending it helped us, though, and during what would turn out to be my final visit to her, I felt no need to press her on the subject.

So, Toby and I and our spouses and kids will go to Islesboro with a knife sharp enough to sever the heavy plastic bags enclosing Mum's ashes, and Dad's ashes, and Jane's. Writing that about the knife and the bags reminds me intensely of when my son needed to be induced. He was well beyond his due date, which in itself didn't worry me, but I had started to leak amniotic fluid, so the amniotic sac was clearly weakening. Pitocin wasn't working to encourage strong contractions, so my doctor reached in and broke the sac, releasing a rush of hot fluid that got Linus moving. It wasn't easy for the doctor to do. I watched the effort on his face as he endeavored to make the break swift and clean. It was painful for me, but it was also astonishing, and brought Linus and me together in a new way. We will do the same for Mum and Dad. We will do the same for Jane.

IF I COULD DO IT ALL AGAIN

There are three things I'd do differently if I had the chance.

One:

I wouldn't throw Mum's teddy bear away when she told me to.

It went mightily against the grain at the time, and the only way I can explain not keeping him for myself is that I was fully into doing-what-Mum-instructed mode. Teddy had been with Mum all her life; she'd even taken him on her honeymoon to Macchu Picchu. He had holes and patches, wonky ears and mismatched eyes in a face that somehow remained as sweet as ever. I kept Poppy, her doll that was almost as old, because I had played with Poppy as a child, but Teddy had always seemed too beat up to play with and I'd kept a respectful distance.

Mum decided that it was time for Teddy to be thrown away when we were going through her belongings before she moved to PRH. It was very interesting to me that she didn't opt to take him there with her, given that he'd been such a constant. Instead, she brought Eric, a much smaller stuffed dog that had been a gift from a friend several years before, and who usually hung out in her wrought-iron bedhead. She really, really didn't want to drag the past with her. She'd rather organize it.

I remember listening to her going through the thinking that led to the decision to have me take Teddy to the trash. He was sitting on her bedroom windowsill, and she was standing about ten feet away, looking at him, deciding that he had served his purpose, unable to imagine that anyone else would want him. It was very uncomfortable putting him in the bag with the clothes too far-gone to give away and it alarms me to think about it now. At the same time, I don't think I could imagine anyone wanting

159

him after I go. But you don't have to be able to imagine that. What you can imagine, and what I do imagine, is Teddy's ignominious end, because it's not an end. He wasn't cremated. He's under some rubbish, I imagine. Sometimes I see him in pieces. I'd really rather not.

Two:

Toby and I both wish we could have helped more with the agitation of those last few days that led to repetitive movements, indicating discomfort we could neither identify nor remedy.

In September 2018, I had written to a friend whose father had died in hideous circumstances and who was haunted and embittered by the memory, "It's terrible that the suffering of our loved ones stays with us, even when they are no longer in pain. Do let it go, just as your poppa has." I wrote to her again, ten months later: "Now I'm back in England, and I find myself thinking often of you, and remembering your pain about how things went at the end of your dad's life, and your mum's. I remember how glibly I advised you to let it go, because they are at peace now. My mum struggled only for a couple of days, but it pains me so much to think about. Thirty seconds is too long. I understand your anguish now."

Could we have had more morphine, Ativan, and Haldol for Mum? Maybe, but probably not. In stressing after she died about her days of struggle, I had the idea that we could have avoided this feeling if we had asked at the outset what the maximum amounts available were. When we'd reached that amount, we wouldn't have spent any time wondering then, or later, if there was more available. But I've learned that people respond so differently to these drugs that the only way to walk the line between calming and terminating is to go case by case, waiting for signs that more is needed before giving it. Once the person dying is no longer conscious, everything is a judgment call, and the line must be guarded. There's no app for this, no chart to plug height and weight and age into to come up with a golden number.

Learning this has actually comforted me – her last days went the way they had to go, but I learned it after the fact. If I could do it all again, I'd speak to more people about the end, to gain a broader understanding of it. There were people with knowledge and experience all around me the whole time. I suppose I thought that Mum's death would resemble Dad's. I certainly hoped it would.

Three:

Within a handful of hours of my father's death, I put up a Facebook post, not thinking about the fact that my mother and I had some mutual friends. This meant that people started getting in touch with her about the loss of her husband before she was ready. I needed my friends to know right away, but Mum needed a quiet moment. If I could do that again, I'd either wait, or put in the post that Mum's friends should wait to hear from her.

The third thing I'd do differently after Mum died also involves the announcement of it, this time in the form of an email we sent out to her friends on the evening of the day she took her leave. Surely it could have waited until morning, but I suppose we thought we were in our right minds. The problem is I'm not great at crossing all the T's at the best of times. The message I sent from my laptop didn't include anything about funeral or memorial arrangements, or that donations to the Pat Roche Hospice Home would be appreciated in lieu of flowers. As a result, we had to field a lot of questions in the next days. I also hit Send before attaching the lovely photo of Mum we'd meant to include, and then sent it out as a second email, which people often saw first and simply thought "What a great photo!" We got some responses saying just that, and then embarrassed follow-up messages when the sender learned, in the next email down, that their friend had died.

D'oh.

A few days after Mum achieved lift-off, I realized that the various bruises on my thighs came from having continually walked into the sharp corners of the footboard of her hospice bed. I spent nine weeks moving around that room, but kept stepping too close to the footboard, at speed, because my eyes were always on Mum, putting the footboard in a blind spot. I could probably have avoided bumping into it if I had slowed down a bit – in fact, I could probably have avoided wishing anything had been different if I had slowed down a bit – but I don't regret bruising myself. It's not something I'd try and do differently, because it was evidence of how I was paying more attention to my mother than to furniture placement. I'm glad I did that. Plus, I had otherwise healed.

In among the stretches of joy and admiration, mental engagement and clowning of our relationship, my mother and I had hurt each other horribly. She could be very caustic, she overshared, she laughed at sore spots.

I could be very caustic, I overshared, I took a very long time to develop any healthy boundaries. At the end of her life, though, Mum made herself comfortable in her hospice bed, covered in a big red blanket she got at a jumble sale and a very finely worked patchwork quilt made by my father's grandmother, and was unwaveringly sweet. So was I. There was no effort in it for either of us, which was astonishing to us both. (Mum said to me several times, "Why are you so *amenable*?", which goes to show you how often she felt I hadn't been.) The monumental gift of the experience of helping her to die is the deep mending that went on in those earlier wounds. Our baggage fell right away, and we were our pre-pain selves.

On the same day that I figured out where the bruises had come from, and despite the aching fatigue of grief, I wrote:

> *The last weeks of spring*
> *Everything dusted ochre*
> *We drive through promise*

ALISON JEAN LESTER is the author of the novels *Lillian on Life* and *Yuki Means Happiness*, and the short story collection *Locked Out: Stories Far from Home*. She spent her early life in the US and the UK, and pursued her higher education in the US, China and Italy. She lived in Japan from 1991 to 1999, working as a freelance writer and voiceover artist, and giving birth to her two children. From 1999 to 2016 she lived in Singapore, where she ran her own communication skills training and coaching business. She now lives in England.

MARY ANN FRYE is a graphic designer and artist. Her career in visual communication has encompassed exhibit design for history and art museums; typographic, symbol and identity design; twenty years teaching; and heading a university program in graphic design. Study of color at the Rhode Island School of Design inspired a parallel passion for painting and most recently completion of a series of 1500 portraits in 1500 consecutive days. She has flown as a private pilot, sailed on a racing crew and, lately, taken ardently to the surf.

These paintings of Alison and Mary Ann are monochrome versions of two from Mary Ann's 1500 portraits project.

ACKNOWLEDGMENTS

Scores of people supported my mother, father, and aunt in their final years, months, and weeks, and supported me as well. I am profoundly grateful to you all for your companionship, camaraderie, and creativity.

The *Absolutely Delicious* team has been absolutely delicious. Thank you, Mary Ann, for the elegant, emotional drawings and all the fascinating conversations that led to their final versions. Thank you, Mike, for the knock-out design and your good-natured reception of all my tweaks and questions. Thank you, Andy, for the peace of your embrace and your enthusiasm for helping with all things devilishly digital.

As you can imagine, reading through the manuscript over and over was emotionally draining. I am indebted to Lesley Dickinson and Jane Joyce for the opportunity to delegate the job to their eagle eyes. Rachael Hardcastle couldn't have been more helpful on how to navigate my way through the publishing landscape.

This book is set in Scala and Scala Sans, a typeface family designed by Dutch type designer, Martin Majoor. Straightforward and distinctive, Scala is a sturdy design that maintains its integrity by minimizing the contrast among the parts of each letter. Scala Sans is derived directly from Scala and retains the warmth and readability of its source, most notably in the italic. The Scala typefaces are well suited for a book that gives voice to such a wide range of texts, from emails and lists to song lyrics and poetry.